THE MINISTRY OF
FOOD

THE MINISTRY OF FOOD

JANE FEARNLEY-WHITTINGSTALL

HODDER &
STOUGHTON

IMPERIAL WAR
MUSEUM

FIRST PUBLISHED IN GREAT BRITAIN

in 2010 by Hodder & Stoughton
An Hachette UK company

1

A CIP CATALOGUE RECORD FOR THIS TITLE IS AVAILABLE FROM THE BRITISH LIBRARY.

ISBN 978 1 444 70035 0

Designed by Georgia Vaux. Type set in Corona, Gill Sans, Caslon 3, Anchor Steam, Britanic, Joga.

Hodder & Stoughton policy is to use papers that are natural, renewable and recyclable products and made from wood grown in sustainable forests. The logging and manufacturing processes are expected to conform to the environmental regulations of the country of origin.

HODDER & STOUGHTON LTD
338 Euston Road
London NW1 3BH
www.hodder.co.uk
www.iwm.org.uk

PRINTED AND BOUND BY BUTLER TANNER AND DENNIS LTD, FROME AND LONDON

For Peter

6 STARS FROM *the* WINTER GARDEN

SAVOY THE BIG-HEARTED TENOR

KALE THE EVER GREEN

IF ITS HEALTH YOU'RE AFTER **CABBAGE** YOU LUCKY PEOPLE

SPINACH
THE STRONGEST MAN IN THE WORLD

THE LEEKS

THEY KNOW THEIR ONIONS

THE SPROUT SISTERS
Very tasty — very sweet

GROW THEM IN *your* WINTER GARDEN

Foreword

I am delighted to write a foreword for this book, and to revive memories of my days in the Ministry of Food. Many people are unaware of the huge task with which the Ministry dealt during the Second World War, when forced to ration basic foods. This book and the Imperial War Museum exhibition held to celebrate the 70th anniversary of rationing recalls the effect it had on everyday lives.

The first section of this book is on 'Digging for Victory'. The expert advice includes facts given during the war years and inspires gardeners to produce a wonderful range of produce for today. The second section is on cooking under the heading of 'The Kitchen Front'. It includes recipes that were popular during the years of rationing, and many that will be popular today. Throughout this section we are reminded that good cooking also means no wastage of food.

The head of the Ministry of Food from 1940 to 1945 was Lord Woolton. Although not a member of a political party he was appointed by the Prime Minister, Neville Chamberlain, who recognised his business ability, but above all his skill in communicating with the general public. This meant an ability to persuade them to accept change and restrictions. I always compared him to a favourite uncle or even Father Christmas – Jane however has taught me something. She refers to Lord Woolton as 'Uncle Fred' she has found people who addressed him as this when writing to the Ministry of Food. 'Uncle Fred' – not very dignified for the head of a mighty Ministry, but very successful.

My colleagues and I were called Food Advisers. All over Britain were Food Advice Centres, staffed by experienced home economists drawn from education and industry. Our job was to help the public keep their families well fed with the ingredients available.

Often I am asked if the Ministry of Food was a success. Without a moment's hesitation I answer 'Yes'. It fought on the Home Front, so played a part in winning the war. Also it kept children and adults healthy throughout the period.

The exhibition and Jane's book prove these points, so I salute both of them.

Marguerite Patten OBE

GARDEN PLOT
to
KITCHEN POT

**GARDEN HINTS
BY THE MINISTRY OF AGRICULTURE
RECIPES
BY THE MINISTRY OF FOOD**

Introduction

The Second World War started on 3 September 1939 and officially ended with VJ (Victory in Japan) day on 15 August 1945. Shortly after it broke out – I was six months old at the time – my grandparents insisted that my mother, her sisters and all their grandchildren came to stay with them on their farm in Wiltshire. There for the next five-and-a-half years we led lives sheltered from the dangers, and many of the deprivations, experienced by most of wartime Britain. My youngest aunt worked on the farm, smart in her Land Girl's uniform, and in summer we all helped in the harvest field where the whole village turned out to stook the sheaves of corn, or heave them onto wagons pulled by plodding carthorses.

Because we lived on a farm and also had the benefit of a large vegetable garden, I was blissfully unaware of rationing until we returned to London when the war ended. It is often forgotten that food shortages continued, and in some respects got worse, in the post-war period. The day when sweets came 'off the ration' in 1953 was a red letter day for us children, but it was not until June 1954 that rationing finally ended when meat and bacon became freely available.

Throughout the years of austerity we ate healthily and took good food for granted. With hindsight, I realise how skilfully my mother and others like her conjured tasty dishes from meagre rations. I realise, too, that these resourceful women could not have fed their families at all without intelligent government planning, masterminded by the Ministry of Agriculture and the Ministry of Food.

There are two parts to the story of wartime food. The first describes the battle to increase food production by changing the agricultural system and encouraging self-help. The Women's Land Army was part of the drive to grow more food, and its work is celebrated in the personal histories of some of the hard-working Land Girls. At a more domestic level, the famous Dig for Victory campaign, urging everyone to give their gardens over to growing vegetables, was a triumph of propaganda.

Some remarkable people were involved in these

initiatives. Lord Woolton was Minister of Food from 1940 until 1943, and when it came to planning and implementing the rationing of food, his attractive personality and flair for publicity made him a popular advocate of unpopular policies.

The second part of the book deals with 'The Kitchen Front,' the title Lord Woolton coined for a daily wireless broadcast about producing healthy meals with limited resources. The battle on the food front was fought largely by women who, with their husbands away at the war, found themselves for the first time in their lives having to make key decisions on their own. Many of them kept diaries, through which, some seventy years later, we can share their lives.

The Imperial War Museum's collections are rich in personal accounts of daily life during the war. Another invaluable resource in preparing this book has been the archive of Mass Observation, an organisation founded in 1937 to study the everyday lives of ordinary people in Britain. Volunteers were recruited by Mass Observation to record their day-to-day lives in diaries. They lived in diverse parts of the country, were of varying ages and had a wide range of different ways of life. Their diaries, written as food shortages developed, and as rations dwindled to subsistence level, describe their wartime experiences vividly. For women, feeding their families was a daily challenge. It was uppermost in their minds and featured prominently in their diaries. Some, like the Lancashire housewife Nella Last, turned out to be gifted writers, and extracts from their diaries feature in other accounts of life during the Second World War. Nella, in particular, was a resourceful manager and an imaginative cook, and the way she produced appetising meals from unpromising ingredients is inspiring.

Delving into the Imperial War Museum's collection to find illustrations for this history of wartime food has been a treat and a revelation. The war coincided with a period of crisp and lively graphic style, and some of the government's posters and leaflets are a visual delight. Together with photographs, quotations from letters and diaries, interviews, popular songs and radio shows, they tell

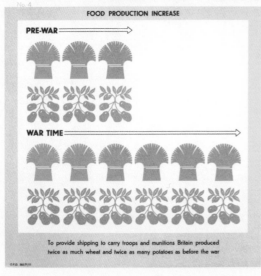

GREAT BRITAIN'S WAR EFFORT

No. 4

FOOD PRODUCTION INCREASE

PRE-WAR

WAR TIME

To provide shipping to carry troops and munitions Britain produced twice as much wheat and twice as many potatoes as before the war

O.P.D. 86/P/171

a success story. By the end of food rationing in 1954, Britain's children were taller and healthier than they had ever been and the gap between rich and poor had narrowed, as far as nutrition was concerned.

We ourselves are now living through a period of unexpected austerity, so can readily recognise and admire the quiet heroism of our mothers and grandmothers as, against the odds, they put meal after nourishing meal on the family table. We can also learn from their good sense and good humour.

Today, instead of fighting Hitler, we are combating economic recession. But, like our forebears, we are fighting on several fronts – against waste, junk food and the depletion of fossil fuels. In hard times the battle for survival can be exhilarating, and it does bring rewards: the satisfaction that comes from self-sufficiency; pride in seeing children grow up strong and healthy; and the friendships that develop through co-operation with neighbours. Apart from enjoying the economic benefits of growing our own food and foraging for wild food, we are fulfilling an instinctive urge to get closer to nature. Even without the stimulus of necessity, there is a strong movement in this direction.

If our mothers and grandmothers could provide good food on a tight budget and with the most basic equipment, it should be much easier for us. Today we have fridges, freezers and kitchen gadgets, not to mention supermarkets. We have spices, herbs and garlic. We may not care to try some of the more bizarre recipes from the rationing era (anyone for Mock Goose, Sheep's Head Roll or Eggless Pancakes?) but others need surprisingly little updating to make delicious meals at very little cost.

Currency

IMPERIAL	DECIMAL
FARTHING (¼ OF A PENNY)	£0.001
HALFPENNY OR HA'PENNY	£0.002
PENNY (240 TO THE POUND)	£0.004
SHILLING (12 PENCE)	£0.05
CROWN (5 SHILLINGS)	£0.25
SOVEREIGN (1 POUND)	£1.00
GUINEA (21 SHILLINGS)	£1.05

SECTION
1

DIG FOR VICTORY

I will not cease from mental fight,
Nor shall my sword sleep in my hand,
Till we have built Jerusalem
In England's green and pleasant land.
  Jerusalem by William Blake

In 1939 the British countryside was still green and pleasant, though not quite the Jerusalem that Blake dreamed of in 1804. Since then, great industrial changes had gradually altered the landscape from an intensively farmed patchwork of small fields to one consisting largely of pasture grazed by cattle and sheep. Britain's rural population, formerly self-sufficient, had migrated to the cities and towns to work among Blake's 'dark, satanic mills': in factories, down coal mines or in the many industries needed to support a manufacturing economy.

Thanks largely to its colonies and dominions, Britain could take advantage of cheap imported food. As a result, more and more farmers had given up growing labour-intensive crops and turned to ranching. By 1939, out of a population of 48 million, only one million people were still employed in agriculture. Home food production declined, and by 1939, more than 60 per cent of Britain's food was imported, much of it from Canada and the USA. Farmers also depended on imports to feed their livestock in winter: cake for their cattle, meal for pigs and corn for hens.

During the First World War the German Navy attempted to prevent vital food supplies reaching Britain – they blockaded merchant ships bringing cargoes to British ports. As a result, food shortages had become a serious problem. The government, aware this could happen again in the event of another European war, had put plans in place for an efficient food distribution system and had accumulated a reserve of agricultural machinery. To that extent Britain was prepared in 1939.

But there had been no increase in domestic food production between the wars, and when it became clear that war was inevitable, this became an urgent priority. Not only were our merchant ships at risk from German U-boats, they were also needed to transport troops, artillery and munitions to war zones.

One hundred acres devoted to the production of beef

THE EMPIRE'S STRENGTH

DO YOU KNOW THAT THE

COLONIES

produce over half the world's
rubber and a third of the tin:
that they are rich in sugar, tea,
coffee, cocoa and fruits: that
Colonial copper, gold and oil
are increasingly important.

THESE ARE THE SINEWS OF WAR

On Sunday, 3 September, 1939 virtually
every household that owned a wireless
tuned in to hear Prime Minister Neville
Chamberlain address the nation: 'I am
speaking to you from the cabinet room
at 10 Downing Street. This morning the
British Ambassador in Berlin handed
the German Government a final note
stating that, unless we heard from them
by 11 o'clock that they were prepared
at once to withdraw their troops from
Poland, a state of war would exist
between us. I have to tell you now that
no such undertaking has been received,
and that consequently this country is at
war with Germany.'

Before the day was out, every War
Ag committee had received a telegram
from the Minister of Agriculture. Each
county was set a target. In Bedfordshire,
for example, the War Ag learnt that they
were expected to convert 10,000 acres
of grassland into arable land. Within
that acreage, specific targets were set,
so many acres of wheat, so many of
potatoes, sugar-beet and so on.

These targets were passed on
from County to District Committees to
Parish representatives, whose job it
was to persuade the farmers to do their
patriotic duty. Apart from patriotism
the incentive was a small government
grant of £2 for every acre of grassland
ploughed up. There was no time to
lose. The grass had to be turned before
winter set in, so that the frost could
break down the clods and clean the
ground of pests. Shortage of tractors was
a major problem (there were just 55,000
in 1939, compared to more than 175,000
by 1944) so cart horses were brought
out of retirement, broken ploughs

or mutton could feed nine people for
a year. The same area producing milk
fed 40. If, instead of keeping livestock,
farmers planted oats, 170 people could
be fed, while a hundred-acre crop of
potatoes could feed 400. Accordingly,
the Ministry of Agriculture devised a
plan to replace grassland with arable
crops, and by the time war was declared
it was ready to swing into action. If a
crop of winter wheat to replace imported bread flour was to be harvested in
the summer of 1940, speedy action was
essential. To implement the plan, War
Agricultural Executive Committees
were set up in each county. Consisting
of farmers and farm worker representatives, they became known as War Ags.

refurbished by village blacksmiths and mildewed leather harnesses cleaned and repaired. County Committees organised machinery and crews to go from farm to farm, and farmers and workers learned to plough not just every hour of daylight, but by moonlight too.

Early in 1940 harsh winter weather brought welcome hard frosts to break up the ground, and by April the national target of 2 million acres sown with winter and spring crops had been achieved.

REGENERATION

The drive to bring more land into production continued by putting together

the most comprehensive land record since the Domesday Book in 1086. The 1940 National Farm Survey was carried out by volunteers in every parish, using 6-inch scale Ordnance Survey maps to survey every holding of more than five acres. Some 300,000 farms were recorded in detail.

Many people's lives were changed. A Peak District farmer, whose three sons had been killed in the First World War had allowed his farm to become derelict and bracken-infested. The War Ag District Committee lent him a tractor... 'I scrubbed up my old plough and cleared 30 acres of bracken that year – alone. I planted wheat, potatoes, and rye – alone... I persuaded my widowed sister to come and live with me, and we got in a Land Girl from the village...Next year I cleared another 10 acres... Now the land's clear; I'm growing rotations of wheat, potatoes, beet and peas... I don't hear anybody saying "poor old George" any more.... I feel like a boy.'

Elsewhere land reclamation was carried out on a far bigger scale than George's 40 acres. Using up-to-date heavy machinery, huge tracts of bog, fen and moorland, never before cultivated, were brought into production. In the Welsh mountains of Montgomeryshire and Radnorshire, following the principle, 'where bracken will grow, potatoes will grow,' bracken and thorn were cleared at the rate of nearly one thousand acres a year. At Dolfor in Radnorshire, enough potatoes were harvested and winter-stored in clamps (mounds of earth and straw) to feed the population of Manchester.

NEW CROPS

Peace-time crops, such as cut flowers, were abandoned. At Helston in Cornwall a farmer who had made his living from 30 acres of spring bulbs remembered, 'You couldn't look at these fields without seeing daffodils, narcissi, anemones, tulips, flowers right down to the cliff edge... Well, there's a different sight to the land now. I ploughed up my bulbs a couple of years back. It wasn't a job I liked doing, I can tell you. Now I'm growing wheat, potatoes, carrots and onions. Some of my bulbs have been steamed and fed to the pigs... Down by the sea I'm growing two crops a year, early potatoes followed by carrots. Weeding's the very devil; the back of my neck is scorched to a cinder, and so is the missus'. Still we can't grumble; we got nearly a hundred sacks of grain last year, 50 tons of potatoes, and 20 of carrots.'

Elsewhere flowers grown under glass, such as lilies and orchids, were replaced by tomatoes and lettuce.

Old, less productive orchards were cleared and ploughed. In others the space between trees was cultivated. A Cambridgeshire farmer with 32 acres of apples, plums and cherries, ploughed the avenues between the rows with a tractor and used a horse-plough for the smaller spaces between each tree. 'I lifted 50 tons [of potatoes] last year,' he reported, 'and I reckon there's half as much again waiting to be lifted.'

Blue-grey lakes appeared in Kent, Sussex and East Anglia. They were lakes not of water but of flax in flower, a new crop grown for the war effort, to make tents, maps, camouflage netting, aircraft fabric and parachute-harnesses.

In Norfolk, 1,500 acres of Feltwell Fen were drained, yielding thousands of tons of rich, black soil. At Swaffham and Burwell in Norfolk, huge trunks of petrified bog-oaks had to be removed. It was decided to dig out around them and blow them up with dynamite. The digging was done with spades – by a hundred Land Girls, mostly from Lancashire. In the Pennines, moorland was ploughed to grow kale, oats, and cattle fodder. In Wiltshire, 500 acres of King's Heath common, where local families had held grazing rights since the time of King Athelstan, grandson of Alfred the Great, was ploughed up for the first time in about a thousand

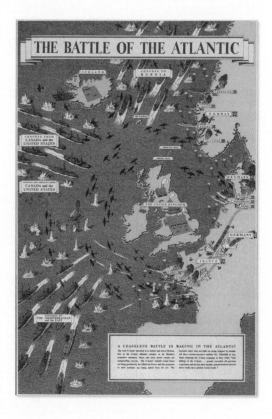

years. A council meeting of commoners was held in the ancient Courthouse of Malmesbury to grant permission.

A long-term result of war-time reclamation of land for agriculture is that today moorland, fens and ancient grassland are scarce and treasured habitats for wildlife, and the conservation of these fragile eco-systems has become of great importance.

SUCCESS

Between 1939 and 1944, 6.5 million new acres had been ploughed, and although 98,000 farm workers had been called up, 117,000 women had replaced them. Between 1939 and 1945 food imports were halved and the acreage of land used to grow food crops increased by 80 per cent. Wheat, barley and potato production had all doubled, and production of oats was up by 58 per cent.

Today we are more interested to know where our food comes from and how it is produced than at any time since the war. Our concerns are different now. We worry about the overuse of chemical fertilisers and pesticides, and we worry about the distance our food has travelled, and the damage these 'food miles' do to the global environment. There is a strong movement toward buying home-grown produce, and as a result people appreciate and enjoy the seasonal changes in their diet. More and more people are growing their own vegetables and fruit, and realise that meat can be enjoyed once or twice a week rather than every day. A wartime diet is not forced upon us as it was upon our grandparents, but we may wish to adapt elements from it for reasons of health and quality of life. In the 21st century our wars are against obesity in children and adults, against waste and against financial constraints.

DIG FOR ...

PLENTY

**GROW FOOD IN YOUR GARDEN
OR GET AN ALLOTMENT**

Down on the Farm

'The landscape is daily becoming browner as farmers
obey the national injunction to 'plough up', and one can
see miles over a stretch of agricultural patchwork right to
the foot of Brown Willy. Farms on the whole round here
appear prosperous, though all the farmers are complaining
about the wartime difficulties of getting enough petrol to
deliver their milk in the mornings and the trials of getting
the cattle in during the blackout.'

Tilly Rice, Cornwall, 28 November 1939

The new landscape of brown earth ribbed with furrows
had become, by harvest time, a sea of golden wheat or
oats, punctuated with fields of green potato tops or lucerne
for winter cattle fodder.

Wheat was needed urgently for bread, and in 1942 Lord
Woolton, Minister of Food, introduced the National Loaf.
Roughly equivalent to today's wholemeal bread, it was less
wasteful and more nutritious than white bread, which was
made illegal. Calcium was added to flour to prevent rickets,
which afflicted some of the women joining the Land Army,
as well as children in deprived areas. However, most people hankered after white bread, and some blamed every
minor ailment on 'this nasty, dirty, dark, coarse, indigest-
ible bread'. But by the end of the war 20 per cent more
bread was being eaten than in 1939. The rumour, passed on
to Lord Woolton at a party, that it was an aphrodisiac, may
have helped.

The face of farming changed completely all across the
country. For example on one farm in the south of England
grew from 100 acres to 116 and acres and saw its arable
acreage increase from 15 acres to 58. Between 1939 and
1944, a work force of two men became one man and one
Land Girl. 85 acres of grass was reduced to 58 acres, and

the forty beef cattle fed on grass and imported cake were changed to twenty milking cows, fifteen young stock and one bull, grazed on grass. Where there were once 800 hens in 1944 there were none, and instead of 350 store pigs fed mainly on imported meal the farm had 25 pedigree sows, a boar and 150 young pigs. Of two horses in 1939, one was retained, the other replaced by a new tractor. The focus of agrocilture was drastically different.

One thing that did not change in farming was the sheer hard work involved. A young woman, who married a farmer from a nearby village in Devon, described their return from a brief honeymoon (three nights in Torquay): 'we had 20 cows to milk, calves to feed and poultry and pigs to muck out. This was to be our life as a young married couple, seven days a week, 6am until dark.'

THE LAND ARMY FIGHTS IN THE FIELDS

In the first two years of the war, 50,000 farm workers were called up to serve in the armed services. Furthermore, 6 million additional acres had been brought into productivity, increasing the workload enormously. The Women's Land Army was summoned to the rescue. Its Director was Lady Denman, whose rallying cry was 'The Land Army fights in the fields. It is in the fields of Britain that the most critical battle of the war may well be fought and won.'

It is certainly no exaggeration to say that without the Land Girls, farmers and their depleted labour force would have been hard pressed to sow and harvest crops from those 6 million extra acres.

There was a real risk of malnutrition, if not starvation, and the resulting effect on morale could well have lost the war. Fortunately, pretty well any work that a man could do, Land Girls did too – from milking, ploughing and weeding, to growing crops and harvesting them.

Although the recruitment campaign made the job out to be more glamorous than it actually was, there was no shortage of girls wanting to exchange life chained to an office desk or factory workbench for one in the open air.

Recruits had to pass a medical, but it was hardly demanding. One girl who wore glasses was unable to read the test sheet. 'Never mind', said the examining doctor, 'I suspect you'd see a charging bull.'

The girls were issued with a uniform of brown corduroy breeches, knee length fawn socks, brown brogue shoes, and a green v-necked jumper over fawn aertex shirt. For work, brown dungarees and Wellington boots were provided. They were billeted in the main farmhouse, in cottages with other labourers, or in hostels with accommodation for anything between six and one hundred girls.

Muriel Green described her first job as a Land Girl in her diary for April 1941. She set off from Norfolk to Dorset to become an apprentice in a garden where five girls and a lady head gardener were employed. 'All girls very nice from Kent, Yorkshire, Letchworth... We live in a charming 'ideal home' old cottage and have a sweet bedroom each, bathroom, kitchen and lounge common-room... Food is sent in ready-cooked from manor house and is plentiful.'

Wages were 28 shillings for a 50-hour

week in summer and 48 hours in winter. This was 10 shillings less than the average farm wage at that time, but their meals as well as accommodation were provided. Their contract guaranteed regular employment, a minimum of one week holiday, and no deductions for sickness or wet weather.

Initially the idea of female workers was none too popular with some farmers. On 17th November 1939, the *Bedfordshire Times* reported: 'All is not well with the Land Girls. Many of them left good jobs to undergo training and now find that farmers are unwilling to engage them. In Bedfordshire there is considerable scepticism about their worth... Perhaps the Land Girls will come into their own later on, but there is no doubt that the scheme has been bungled and that some of the girls are bitter about it. For reasons of patriotism many have given up careers only to find that their services are not wanted.'

A market gardener told the same newspaper that Land Girls would be no use for growing onions. 'I don't think the Land Girls would stand the crawling,' he said.

Sometimes, male farm workers resented the girls. At one market garden the foreman gave orders that if any man assisted any Land Girl, the time they spent would be docked from their wages. One wet day, two girls got a fully laden cart stuck in clay soil. It was too heavy to shift, and the girls, tired and a little tearful , appealed to the men for help. They refused.

Many of the 90,000 Land Girls who signed up did find the work extremely hard, the conditions harsh and the hours long. Some had no idea what was expected of them. One girl was sent to work on a dairy farm. She didn't know one end of a cow from another, and in her first week was handed a bucket of soapy water by the cowman and told to wash down the cow he had just milked. He got on with the milking, then turned to see her washing the cow from head to foot, instead of just the udders.

But in spite of their aching bones, callouses and chilblains at the end of a day that usually started at 6am, many city girls took to farming with zest, relishing the novelty of country life and enjoying their new skills. After her first month Muriel Green wrote. 'I am now used to working in the garden all day and must say I love it. I adore the sun and the fresh air. It has been a rest cure. That is a rest from the war. I have worked harder than ever before.'

One 19-year-old young woman from Leicester discovered she had talent as a rat catcher. After brief training she was sent to work in Yorkshire where, in two days, she killed 327 rats in a grain store. As 300 rats can eat 3 tons of wheat in a year, she had saved enough to make thousands of National Loaves.

One aspect of life on the land that appealed to many girls was the freedom from family constraints. This could cause problems for the voluntary organisers who were responsible for the girls' general welfare. In one case a farmer came to see the local organiser about a Land Girl who had gone home at the end of a working day and, by noon the next day, had not returned. When interviewed, the girl said she had returned to the farm so late at night that she had hidden in the Dutch barn, and didn't dare come out the next day.

lend a hand on the land

at a farming holiday camp

She wouldn't say why she was so late getting back.

On another occasion, news went round that an 18-year-old Land Girl was engaged to an Italian Prisoner of War aged 20. 'Her mother is heartbroken,' said one gossip. Another suggested the girl must have felt sorry for the young prisoner. 'Oh no,' said the first, 'with these young girls it's anything in trousers.' 'The Italians are wonderful lovers,' was the reply. 'That's it. The Land Girls go down like ninepins before them.'

PRISONERS OF WAR

Wonderful lovers or not, both Italian and German prisoners of war made a significant contribution to British farming. In Cambridgeshire in 1941, Italian PoWs cleared 100 acres of scrub and brambles, digging drains and cutting down thorn bushes – work which one man said he much preferred to military service in the Libyan desert. Gyro-tillers and bulldozers followed and the work was completed by teams of Land Girls working in shifts so that the tractors were constantly on the move, ploughing, rolling and harrowing until the land was ready to seed.

The relationship between farming families and PoWs was invariably friendly. Two Germans, Joel and Raymond, came to work at a farm near Colyton in Devon. 'Mum felt sorry for them,' Queenie Collier remembers. 'She would make them apple cakes and pies to have with their meals... They were nice boys.'

German and Italian prisoners were held in camps, and were delivered to local farms by truck each morning and collected at teatime. Most were very young and some came from a farming background, so felt at home and were particularly useful. Homesick lads were happy to participate in family life, and showed their appreciation by playing with the farm children, and making toys for them from pieces of wood and other oddments.

LEND A HAND ON THE LAND

Farming families took it for granted that everyone in the family would play their part, especially at such busy times as hay making and harvest, and in rural communities the tradition of helping with harvest extended beyond the immediate family to village neighbours.

During the war there was extra pressure all the year round, and Women's Institutes organised part-time work for volunteers who could spare time from housework. They provided relief milkers and helped with calving so that cowmen and Land Girls could have a day off now and then.

School children from both state and private schools were willing helpers during the holidays, living under canvas or in requisitioned premises. Besides helping with the corn harvest, boys planted and lifted potatoes, drove tractors, pulled flax, and hoed roots. Girls did potato planting and lifting, flax-pulling, weeding, pea-picking and fruit-picking.

In term-time boys over the age of ten were allowed two half days off from school in order to work on farms – much more fun than sitting in a classroom. They even got paid, and could save up their earnings for a bicycle, or, if they were really ambitious, a motorbike. In Scotland many schools closed altogether in October so that pupils could lift and store the potatoes before November frosts.

Dennis Moss and his twin brother, both aged 13, lived in Colyton. 'We had all manner of schemes to put food on our plates and a little money in our pockets. If we bought a hundredweight of seed potatoes, the farmer would allow us a patch of land in which to plant them. He would look after them along with the rest of his crop, and at harvest time we would collect the potatoes. With the farmer's permission, we would also pull up turnips from the fields. In return the farmer would get our help at haymaking and harvest. In orchards we got 6d a bag for apples we knocked from the trees and 3d or 4d for those that had fallen.'

Colyton was also host to one hundred children evacuated from St Jude's School in Southwark, London. 'We had never seen cows, nor even a green hill,' Denis Swann remembers, '... Two afternoons a week we walked up to the school allotment at the top of Sidmouth Road for our contribution to the Dig for Victory effort. Everyone enjoyed that.'

In 1942 boys and girls all over the country worked a total of nearly 10 million hours in the fields, and still more in 1943.

Adults also volunteered to spend their holidays working on farms, and at harvest time there was an exodus of factory workers, civil servants, bank clerks, solicitors, typists, and shop assistants from towns and cities. Most stayed in camps and hostels, or in village halls and schools requisitioned by the Ministry of Agriculture and the Ministry of Labour, and equipped with bunks and kitchens. Pay was a shilling an hour regardless of age or experience.

Maggie Joy Blunt wrote in her diary, 'It was a good holiday. We stayed on a farm at Crossdale, near Ennerdale. We fed on butter and cream and large starchy meals and became liverish. No fruit, few greens or salads. Farm people have no excuse for these sort of shortages but they were they type who do not consider greens or brown bread important... 5 dogs, 10 cats, cows, a bull, pet lambs, chickens, every farm animal you can think of.'

From 1942 to 1944 a combination of fine weather, good organisation and spirited enthusiasm, ensured bumper harvests. The various schemes to bring workers to the countryside, and the accompanying publicity campaigns, really did pay dividends.

Today the link between town and country is gathering strength again. Families who can no longer afford to spend their holidays abroad are beginning to realise that their local countryside has much to offer. The Right to Roam gives walkers access to ravishingly beautiful landscapes. Farming is currently not a lucrative industry and many farmers supplement their income by providing bed and breakfast for holidaymakers (and what breakfasts! Home-cured bacon if you are lucky, and new-laid eggs.) Others open their farms to visitors, and sell their produce at the farm gate. In many towns the seasonal produce that, even in wartime, used to be taken for granted, is again available in farmers' markets.

THEY CAN'T RATION THESE

'Run, rabbit, run, rabbit, run, run, run
Don't give the farmer his fun, fun, fun
He'll get by without his rabbit pie
So run, rabbit, run, rabbit, run, run, run'

From 'Run Rabbit Run' by Noel Gay and
Ralph Butler, 1939

For most country people, especially those on good terms with a farmer or two, rabbits and wild pigeons were quite easy to get hold of. Not so pheasants, partridges and hares, which as game were protected, though with many gamekeepers away at the war, poaching became a little easier. Rabbits, however, were fair game all the year round.

In towns, rabbit hutches began to appear in back gardens, while in the country, where fields and woods were riddled with rabbit warrens, ferreting became a lucrative sideline. A typical bag would be 20–30 rabbits at two shillings apiece. At harvest time, the mechanical reaper would start cutting the corn on the outside of the field, and as it progressed, the rectangle of uncut corn at the centre would get smaller and smaller. Finally, a ring of men and boys armed with guns and sticks would surround the last patch and as the final swathes were cut, dozens of rabbits would run out and the air would be thick with shooting and shouting and thwacking.

Rabbits can be fed on

Hedgerow Weeds · Garden Waste · Kitchen Scraps

Hedge Parsley	Brussels Sprout Stems	Pot Scrapings
Plantain	Lettuce Leaves	Table Scraps
Sow Thistle	Cabbage Leaves	Root Peelings
Dandelion	Waste Potatoes	Fish Waste
Groundsel	Lawn Mowings	Pea Pods

RABBIT PIE

Serves 6

Initially there was some resistance among city-dwellers to eating the fluffy little bunnies they'd seen scampering in fields on country walks, but when meat was strictly rationed and chickens became hard to come by, such scruples were easier to overcome. Soon roast rabbit, rabbit stew and rabbit pie appeared regularly on both town and country tables. Today there is still some lingering dubiousness about eating rabbit, but it really is a most delicious meat, especially in a pie.

25g (1oz) butter
1 large onion, sliced
1 rabbit, cut into six joints
300ml (10½ fl oz) chicken stock
225g (8oz) ham or bacon, diced
8 pitted prunes
1 tablespoon plain flour

3 tablespoons double cream
2 tablespoons parsley, chopped
salt and freshly ground black
  pepper
225g (8oz) puff or shortcrust
  pastry

Melt half the butter in a saucepan, add the onion and cook gently until translucent. Add the rabbit joints and turn in the butter for a few minutes. Add enough stock to just cover the meat, and simmer gently for 45 minutes.

Preheat the oven to 180°C (350°F) gas mark 4.

Leave the rabbit to cool in the stock then transfer the pieces to a pie dish with the ham or bacon and prunes.

Melt the rest of the butter, stir in the flour and cook for a minute without allowing it to colour. Add the stock, stirring all the time until smooth. Add the cream and parsley. Taste and season with salt and pepper.

Pour the sauce over the rabbit.

Roll out the pastry and lay it over the dish. Press down the edges using your thumbs or the back of a fork. With the tip of a sharp knife make a whole in the centre of the pie to allow steam to escape, and bake for about an hour, until golden. The pie can be eaten hot or cold.

Tip: If you want the rabbit meat to be particularly white and of delicate flavour (i.e. if you want to pretend it's chicken), before cooking, soak the joints for a few hours in water with a teaspoon of vinegar added per pint of water. Alternatively, just use chicken instead of rabbit.

NETTLE SOUP

Serves 6

Today we are rediscovering the delights of food for free, experimenting with recipes for nettle soup, herby sorrel to serve with fish, elderflower cordial and rowan jelly.

½ carrier bag of nettles, tops or young leaves
55g (2oz) butter
I large onion, finely sliced
I large garlic clove, peeled and crushed
I large potato, peeled and diced

I litre (I ³/₄ pints) chicken stock
4 tablespoons double cream
salt and freshly ground black pepper
a bunch of chives

Wearing rubber gloves to protect your hands, pick over the nettles discarding any tough stalks. Wash the nettles thoroughly.

Melt the butter in a large saucepan and cook the onion gently until transparent.

Add the garlic, potatoes and stock. Bring to the boil and simmer until the potatoes are soft. Add the nettles and simmer for a further 5–10 minutes until they are tender. Season with salt and pepper.

Purée the soup in a blender. Return to a clean saucepan, stir in half the cream and reheat. Check the seasoning, pour into bowls, add a swirl of cream and, using scissors, snip a garnish of chives on top.

They Can't Ration These was the title of a timely cookery book by the Vicomte de Maudit, published in 1940. The Vicomte, an early advocate of self-sufficiency, explained in his Preface, 'The object of this book is to show where to seek and how to use Nature's larder, which in time of peace and plenty people overlook or ignore... And when Peace will again come on Earth, the people of Britain, already made conscious through food rationing that meals no longer consist of a hot and then cold "joint with two veg.," will find this book a practical and valuable guide to better things.'

David Lloyd George, Britain's Prime Minister at the end of the First World War, endorsed the book as 'a valuable contribution towards our national defence'.

These days the idea of foraging for wild fruits, fungi and the like has become familiar to us through television programmes and books as a leisure pursuit, but during the war nature's larder was an important source of food that was not only off the ration but also free.

I doubt if many enthusiasts, then or now, would rush to try the Vicomte's recipes for Clover Purée or Roasted Hedgehog, but he had plenty of suggestions for cooking game and all sorts of wild greens, including nettles, sorrel, dandelions and yarrow.

'Nettles are nutritive as well as health-giving. They are a blood purifier and a cure for rheumatism and insomnia. When gathering nettles it is well to protect the hands and legs, but if stung, the best remedy is to rub the affected part with a bruised dock leaf, which Nature provided to be found wherever the nettle grows.' (*They Can't Ration These* by Vicomte de Mauduit)

There was not much traffic on country roads even in peace time, and during the war petrol rationing meant that you were more likely to meet a horse than a car. So you could feel safe and take your time gathering the hedgerow harvest. A stroll down any country lane would yield fruits, nuts, salads and herbs, and many people would never dream of setting out for a walk without a bag or basket.

On the coast sea birds nesting in rocky cliffs, especially gulls, proved an irresistible challenge to adventurous boys. They risked life and limb scrambling down the cliff face to rob the nests. Local fishmongers would pay as much as half a crown (2s 6d) per egg. The eggs would then be packed in boxes and sent to London, where demand was great.

Wild berries and fruits, if not eaten immediately, were made into preserves and rosehips were converted into a health-giving syrup. Blackberries and crab apples, together or separately, became jam or jelly, or were bottled to keep for a winter compote or pie filling.

Sometimes there was competition for nature's bounty. Someone else would have got up earlier and stripped the bushes. One town-dweller on holiday in the country, having picked a big basket of ripe blackberries, searched in vain for mushrooms. She met a small local boy who told her, 'They soldiers do be getting up before it's light and going for mushrooms and berries.'

Once again we are cooking such well-loved favourites as blackberry and apple or wild plum puddings, pies, tarts and crumbles.

BLACKBERRY & APPLE PUDDING

Serves 6–8

This wartime staple remains just as popular today. This ranks high as comfort food in the season of mists and mellow fruitfulness. During the war it would have seemed worth saving up your sugar ration to make it. Then, it might have been served with custard made with dried egg. Now, I'd have cream, the thicker the better. The proportion of apples to blackberries can be varied: if you have plenty of blackberries, use fewer apples.

for the suet pastry:
225g (8oz) self-raising flour
1 level teaspoon salt
115g (4oz) suet
2–3 tablespoons cold water

for the filling:
675g (1lb 8oz) cooking apples,
   peeled, cored and sliced
175g (6oz) blackberries
115g (4oz) sugar

Grease a 1.3 litre/2¼ pint pudding basin. Sift the flour and salt into a bowl, add the suet and mix. Add cold water, a little at a time, until the dough holds together.

Roll out the pastry on a floured surface and use it to line the pudding basin with a slight overlap, cutting out a wedge to make it fit. Squidge up the surplus wedge and roll it out again to make the lid.

Put the apples and blackberries into the basin in layers, sprinkling each layer with sugar. Brush the edges of the pastry with water, put on the lid and seal carefully.

Cover the top with greaseproof paper or foil, tying it down with string. Put the basin in a saucepan and pour in boiling water to reach half way up the sides. Boil for 2½ hours, topping up with water from the kettle as necessary.

To turn the pudding out, remove the greaseproof paper or foil, ease a palette knife down the sides of the basin to loosen the pudding, put a deep plate or shallow dish over the top and up-end it. Be extremely careful as the filling is very hot and will burn you if it leaks out. After a sharp tap or two, the basin will come away, leaving the pudding intact. Eat it with custard or thick cream and extra sugar if needed.

Variation: Fill the pudding with any fruit that happens to be in season.

DIG FOR VICTORY

'The Little Man with the Spade'

'We want not only the big man with the plough but the little
man with the spade to get busy this autumn... Let Dig for
Victory be the motto of everyone with a garden.'
*BBC Radio broadcast by Robert Hudson, Minister for
Agriculture, 10 September 1940*

'**D**ig for Victory' was the slogan of one of the most
successful advertising campaigns ever created in
Britain. Designed to thwart Germany in its plan to starve
Britain into surrender by attacking the convoys of ships
bringing food from abroad, it called on citizens and
communities to use every square foot of spare land to grow
food at home.

The scheme was initiated by Sir Reginald Dorman-Smith,
Minister of Agriculture and Fisheries from January 1939
until May 1940, but when Winston Churchill became
Prime Minister Dorman-Smith was not reappointed
and the Dig for Victory campaign was taken over by his
successor, Robert Hudson. Credit must also go to the Labour
MP Tom Williams, who was Hudson's deputy and himself
became Minister of Agriculture and Fisheries after the
1945 General Election.

Dig for Victory was supported by a series of striking
posters, and more than a million leaflets distributed from
local centres. Coverage was so thorough that, among other
publicity material sent to local councils by the Ministry,
were 4,700 copies of Some Notes for Sermons, 'in case local
authorities might ask local clergymen to mention Dig for
Victory from the pulpit'.

The campaign was a huge success from the start. Its
efficient organisation was the work of Professor John
Raeburn, an engineer's son, born in Kirkcaldy in Scotland,

and a respected agricultural economist. Raeburn joined the Ministry of Food in 1939 and, although Lord Woolton, the Minister of Food from 1940 to 1943, is often credited with masterminding Dig for Victory, it was Raeburn who ran it for most of the war.

He made sure that land was released for allotments, and that information was available to those who had never gardened before. Moreover, he practised what he preached, growing enough vegetables to feed his family throughout his life. The healthy lifestyle stood him in good stead, and he lived to the age of 93. His canny Scottish frugality led him to follow another Ministry of Food campaign, the war against waste, in exemplary fashion. He is said to have been meticulous about saving for re-use

the string with which he tied his bean poles, and to have re-used envelopes many times over.

ALLOTMENTS

There has been a long tradition in Britain of local councils making plots available to town-dwellers who had no gardens, and in 1939 there were already some 815,000 allotments. Under the direction of the Dig for Victory organisers, the population set to with a will to create many more. Parks, football pitches, race courses, golf courses, tennis courts, road verges and railway embankments were dug over. By 1943 the total number of allotments had risen to 1,400,000 and nearly a million tonnes of vegetables were harvested in the peak years of production.

Wartime vegetable growers, both old hands and new recruits, took pride and pleasure in their work. Nella Last in Barrow, Lancashire, wrote in her diary for 5 Sept 1942, 'It was six o'clock before we had tea and I had a plate of lovely sliced tomatoes – picked fresh off my own two plants. I must try next year to have more for they have been such a good thing. Ripening slowly I've picked one or two off as they were ready and not had them all on the dish and had to "use up all at once" before they went bad.'

Herbert Brush, a 70-year-old allotment holder living with friends in Forest Hill, London, also kept a wartime diary. He found working on the allotment therapeutic, and recorded, 'My stiff neck is feeling better since I did a little gardening this morning.' Like Nella Last, he was proud of the fruits of his labour, and wrote, 'There is not a square foot on my allotment now which has not something or other planted on it; and I still have scores of plants growing and just ready to plant out, with no space available. As it is, I have crowded things so that they will have scarce room to grow.'

The allotments were sociable places. Herbert Brush wrote that the old father of one of the plot-holders was inclined to recount his life history; 'Not a very exciting life as he had been a milkman all the time, but he hinted that he had seen all sides of life, especially in the early mornings.' On another occasion Herbert was visited by an Air Raid Precautions (ARP) worker, who claimed to have grown leeks in Northumberland 14in round and 9 or 10in long. He confessed to having bought six loads of farm manure to achieve this, so Herbert decided, with manure at 20s a load, not to emulate him.

Gardening can be a frustrating business. Herbert found that none of the allotment holders on his site had any success growing onions or lettuces from seed. 'There must be something in the ground,' he wrote, 'but so far we have not found out for certain what it is. It is not wireworm but some other enemy to the Diggers for Victory.'

But there were worse enemies than wireworm. 'W. [a friend] and I went round to look at the allotment, but it was a case of looking for the allotment. Four perches out of the five are one enormous hole and all my potatoes and cabbages have vanished. Apparently the bomb fell on the footpath between two allotments and when it exploded had preference for mine, although I must say that there is not much left of

Hardy's and the plot on the other side of mine has a huge pile of earth on it. The result is that all my work there has been wasted, absolutely wasted' (Herbert Brush, October 1940).

If war can ever be said to generate bonuses, one bonus of Dig for Victory (and wartime in general) was the spirit of co-operation it engendered. Maggie Joy Blunt, a Mass Observation diarist, wrote on 7 March 1942, 'A soldier has dug my two cabbage patches for me. He is stationed in this area and seems to get quite a bit of free time in which he comes to aid the gardener-less folk around here.' Allotment holders were also generous in sharing their surplus seeds and plants, and their expertise.

LANDSHARE

Dig for Victory is strikingly relevant again today, when so many people are keen to grow their own food, albeit for rather different reasons. Then, it was a necessity, a patriotic duty that people were glad to perform, as it made them feel that they were making an important contribution to the war effort. This time around, the enemies are climate change, the credit crunch and junk food rather than German U-boats, but, like wartime gardeners and allotment holders, those who grow their own discover a new and fulfilling sense of purpose. There is plenty of media coverage today of the swelling grow your own movement. People are discovering that growing, cooking and eating your own food saves money, keeps the whole family fit and is an ecologically sound way to live.

People with back gardens are digging up their lawns and flower beds to grow vegetables, just as their grandparents did during the war, while those without gardens find space on roofs and balconies and in window boxes to grow a few peas, beans and salads. Of the 1,400,000 wartime allotments, just 250,000 remain today. Meanwhile, more than 100,000 people are on the waiting lists for any that become vacant, and the queue is still growing.

People are hungry for land, and in 2007 a new concept was born to meet the demand. Landshare is a scheme covering the whole of the UK. The idea is that people or organisations with land to spare will make it available to local communities and individuals who want to grow their own fruit and vegetables. One such organisation is the National Trust, which has donated 1,000 plots on its own properties, in the restored kitchen gardens of historic houses, on agricultural land or on vacant land adjacent to Trust properties. They vary in size, from small plots for growers new to the game, to larger areas suitable for community groups, such as schools, charities and clubs. Even the back garden of the Trust's central London office in Queen Anne's Gate has become an allotment used by staff.

Digging up your garden lawn or getting your own plot is only the beginning. Advice is essential, especially for city-dwellers who have never gardened before, and with that in mind an army of 'veg doctors' has been recruited with the help of the Royal Horticultural Society, the charity Garden Organic, and the National Trust. As experienced gardeners, the veg doctors are available to hold the hands (or spades or forks) of beginners, pass on their skills and knowledge and advise on what to grow where, when and how.

In the computer age the Landshare scheme is a good deal easier to administer than it would have been in the Dig for Victory days. An online matchmaking database can link keen growers with landowners at the touch of a button and expert advice is available by picking up the telephone or going online.

KEEPING LIVESTOCK

'... blessing my hens and garden many times a day when I've eggs in water glass to cook with, one hen laying for the table, cockerels to think of for wonderful "pre-war" lunches and my 11 strong vigorous little pullets growing up rapidly and all being well to start laying by the end of October. I'd be more "self-supporting" if I'd more room – it's grand to feel "independent" of shops and rationing' (Nella Last's Diary).

The Ministry of Food encouraged people to rear livestock in their back gardens, as well as growing vegetables. Hens were popular, as fresh eggs were scarce and their allocation controlled, and dried egg – imported from the USA – was disliked. You could make a cake with dried egg and, at a pinch, you could scramble it, but you couldn't poach, boil or fry it. So a fresh egg from your own hen for breakfast was a blessing.

An additional blessing for poultry keepers was the occasional hen past her laying best. She may have been nothing better than an 'old boiler', but almost any meat was welcome. Diarist Ernest van Someren, a research chemist living in Hertfordshire with his wife and two children, killed his oldest hen because she had not been laying for some time. As the butcher was too busy, his wife plucked and cleaned the bird. She had never done it before, but she managed by following the instructions in a magazine article. They ate the hen for Sunday lunch: 'a bit tough but tasty'.

In town terraces as well as country villages, a rabbit hutch at the bottom of the garden was not an unusual sight. Rearing rabbits for the pot, or to sell to the butcher, should have been easy, since their food could be supplemented with kitchen scraps and garden weeds, and they fattened up quickly. The trouble was, it was difficult to stop children making pets of the rabbits and then, when it was time to put poor bunnikins into a pie, there would be anguished tears.

WASTE NOT

'Those who have the will to win
Cook potatoes in their skin,
Knowing that the sight of peelings,
Deeply hurts Lord Woolton's feelings.'
Ministry of Food advertisement

All food that could reasonably be considered fit for human consumption was eaten, and any remaining vegetable peelings, outside leaves of lettuces and cabbages, even tea leaves, were saved to feed chickens, rabbits or pigs, or to make garden compost.

The Ministry of Food launched a strong campaign of posters and short cinema films urging people to Waste Not Want Not. As well as kitchen refuse, householders were asked to salvage everything they might, in normal times, have thrown away. Paper, rags, metal, rubber and bones (to be washed before you put them out) were sorted into separate boxes or tied in bundles, and left on the pavement to be collected for recycling. It may surprise modern recyclers to find bones on the list; they were boiled down to make glue, which was used in aircraft manufacture, or ground up for use as fertiliser, or made into glycerine for high explosives for shells and bombs. According to Advertisers' Weekly, a single chop bone weighing 2oz

THE EFFECTS OF OVER-COOKING AND KEEPING HOT

Vitamin value, goodness, taste
'go up in smoke'—result is waste

could supply two rounds of ammunition for RAF Hurricane fighter guns. Some local authorities organised their own appeals: in Rochdale, householders were requested to 'Please Save All Bones, even those the dog has gnawed, (but not fish bones) and put them in the communal bone bins.'

Nothing, the Government urged, should go to waste. Some households kept goats, which acted as an extra dustbin, converting kitchen refuse into milk and cheese. The Ministry of Food did all they could to encourage pig keeping, since pigs are the ultimate efficient recyclers of kitchen waste. Some nine hundred 'pig clubs' were formed, and people would take their kitchen scraps to communal waste bins, to be fed to the pigs. Gwen Millward, a child

in Leamington Spa during the war, explained 'Dotted around everywhere were dustbins. Our nearest one was on Church Hill under a big tree. Everyone used to put their scraps, potato peelings and such in these bins, and they were used to feed livestock.'

'Because of the pail, the scraps were saved,
Because of the scraps, the pigs were saved,
Because of the pigs, the rations were saved,
Because of the rations, the ships were
    saved,
Because of the ships, the island was saved,
Because of the island, the Empire was
    saved,
And all because of the housewife's pail.'
Ministry of Food advertisement

Pigs are sociable creatures, and don't thrive if they are kept in solitary confinement. For those who kept a pig in their garden, the rule was that a second pig had to be reared with it and this would be given to the Ministry of Food. It was not unusual to bend the rules and keep a third pig. One householder kept a pig for his own family's consumption, gave one to the Ministry, then set about delivering the various portions of the third pig to his friends. The nature of his deliveries dictated that they should be undertaken under the cover of darkness, and the easiest mode of transport was the baby's pram. He had not been out long before he met the local policeman doing his rounds. They stopped to chat and the Bobby commented on the fact that he was out late with the baby. His reply was that he was walking the baby to get him off to sleep. To his great relief the Bobby did not look inside the pram, and he completed his mission successfully.

People who keep pigs tend to develop respect for them, and some become very fond of them. At least one pig-lover thought the government issue of waste food compound and fish meal was not good enough for his animals. He cooked fresh vegetables specially for his pigs, and mixed them with corn meal. Additional treats such as lemon curd waste from the local jam factory and waste cake and bread from the baker ensured that they produced the best bacon and ham for miles around.

MAKING THE MOST OF A GLUT

'In nearly all the homes I have been in this last week there has been a great deal of jam-making and fruit-bottling; the crop of gooseberries and currants has been good, and now that it has rained there will be at least a few raspberries. These things will doubtless be scarcer than ever this winter, so everyone who has any fruit is preserving it somehow or other' (Edward Stebbing 12th July 1941).

Everyone who grows vegetables and fruit knows that, even with the most careful planning, supplies fluctuate wildly between feast and famine. In January, when you've dug your last parsnip, there's nothing to eat until the purple sprouting broccoli sprouts, towards the end of February if you're lucky, but more likely in March. On the other hand, in the summer and early autumn, you have your work cut out keeping up with an endless supply of beans, tomatoes and lettuce.

As for fruit, the summer harvest of gooseberries, black, red and white currants and raspberries, followed by plums and damsons, apples and pears, can be overwhelming, not to mention the wild blackberries, plums, crab apples, elderberries and sloes to be gathered in the countryside. It seems almost criminal to let the birds, wasps and slugs have them.

The Government did their bit in encouraging people to preserve the summer and autumn bounty for use in the lean winter months. Among the subjects covered in a set of free Dig for Victory leaflets were Jam and Jelly Making and Drying, Salting, Pickles, Chutneys.

One of home economist Marguerite Patten's responsibilities was supervising fruit preservation sessions at a food centre at Ipswich. Her job was to see that the jams and other

preserves conformed to Ministry of Food standards. The centre covered a part of East Anglia renowned for its fruit growing industry and the sessions did not always go smoothly, 'for most ladies were experienced housewives, with their own very definite ideas on how jams should be made; some wanted to use their own recipes and addressed me firmly. "Young woman, I was making jam before you were born."'

Today, when there's a glut of ripe fruit, it's easy enough to stock up the freezer with whole raspberries to be brought out at Christmas, with fruity mousses and ice creams, and gently stewed fruits to be thawed for winter tarts, pies and crumbles. But in the 1940s nobody had a freezer and few households a fridge; people used traditional methods to preserve the summer glut.

Why bottle fruit when you can easily freeze it? There are at least two good reasons. Bottled fruit is instantly available; you don't have to wait for it to defrost. Some fruits, peaches and apricots for example, and cherries, retain their natural flavour and shape better when preserved in this way. The best reason is that, unlike the plastic boxes or bags of fruit hidden at the bottom of the freezer, the jars of fruit will give you a smug, warm glow every time you see them. There are still few domestic sights more satisfying than a row of sealed glass jars on a shelf, filled with green-golden gooseberries, amber and garnet

BOTTLE *FRUITS...*

Most fruits can be preserved without sugar in sealed jars. Full details are given in "Dig for Victory" Leaflet No. **11**

Apples, pears and stone fruits may be DRIED— Leaflet No. **14** tells you how to do it.

Apples and un-ripe tomatoes may also be wrapped in paper and stored in a dark cupboard.

plums, and ruby raspberries. For this alone it's worth investing in a few of the special jars required for bottling. You can use Kilner jars, which have metal or glass lids sealed with special rubber rings and a metal screw band around the neck, or Le Parfait jars with a glass lid, a rubber ring and a metal spring clip. Both kinds come in ½ litre (17fl oz) and 1 litre (35fl oz) sizes, and replacement lids and rubber rings can be bought separately.

Fruit can be bottled without the addition of sugar, which meant that during the war none of the precious sugar ration need be used. But bottling in syrup improves the flavour of the fruit, and nowadays sugar is plentiful.

HOW TO BOTTLE FRUIT

Syrup: the strength of the syrup you use will depend on how sharp the fruit is. Damsons and rhubarb need a heavy syrup, 250g (9oz) sugar to 600ml (21fl oz) water. 175g (6oz) sugar to 600ml (21fl oz) water is a medium, general purpose syrup. To prepare, dissolve the sugar in the water, bring to the boil and boil for one minute.

1. Preheat the oven to 150°C (300°F) gas mark 2.

2. Put the clean, warm jars 5cm (2in) apart on a baking tray lined with newspaper. Pack the fruit into the jars, using the handle of a wooden spoon to push it in if necessary.

3. Bring the syrup to the boil and pour it over the fruit up to 2.5cm (1in) from the top of the jar.

4. Place the lids on top of the jars but not the clips or screw bands. **5.** Put in the oven and leave for the recommended time (see below):

6. Take the jars out of the oven one at a time and secure the lids with clips or screw bands. Leave for 24 hours and test the seal of the lids by removing the clips or screw bands and lifting the jars carefully by the lids. If they remain tight, the seal is secure. If the lid comes away, either re-process the fruit or eat it immediately.

7. Replace the clips or screw bands, label and store in a cool, dark place.

Bottling fruit times

Apples 30–40 minutes

Apricots 40–50 minutes

Blackberries 30–40 minutes

Cherries 40–50 minutes

Currants 40–50 minutes

Damsons 40–50 minutes

Gooseberries 30–40 minutes

Peaches 50–60 minutes

Pears 60–70 minutes

Plums 45–50 minutes

Raspberries 30–40 minutes

Rhubarb 30–40 minutes

SPICED PEACHES

Makes 2 x 500ml (17fl oz) jars

Once you have mastered the basic system of bottling, you can add liqueurs or flavour the syrup with herbs and spices. My mother used to make delicious spiced peaches to eat with cold meats, especially ham. They are also good with hot ham, bacon, gammon, or duck.

400g (14oz) sugar
300ml (101/2fl oz) white wine
    vinegar
25g (1oz) root ginger, crushed

5cm (2in) cinnamon stick
1 teaspoon allspice berries
1 teaspoon cloves
1kg (2lb 4oz) peaches

To make the spiced syrup put all the ingredients except the peaches into a saucepan. Stir over a low heat until the sugar has dissolved, then boil for one minute.

To peel the peaches, pour boiling water over them and leave for one minute. Remove with a slotted spoon and plunge into cold water. After 30 seconds, the skins will slip off easily.

Halve the peaches, and remove the stone. Gently poach the peach halves in the spiced syrup for 3 minutes before removing them from the syrup. Pack the peach halves carefully into sterilised jars.

Boil the syrup again and strain it over the peaches in the jars.

Cover the jars with vinegar-proof lids (ones with plastic lining). Keep for at least a month before eating, and use within one year.

ROASTED TOMATO PASSATA

Makes 2 x 500ml (17fl oz) jars

In a good year, even a few tomato plants will yield more fruit than the average family can eat without tiring of them. The surplus can be bottled successfully, but the Italian way of preserving them as passata yields an intensely flavoured purée to serve with pasta, and add to sauces, soups and casseroles. Although wartime cooks would not have made passata, bottling is a great example of how a traditional technique can be adapted for today. Roasting the tomatoes with herbs, shallots and garlic is optional but adds greatly to the flavour.

2kg (4lb 8oz) ripe tomatoes
200g (7oz) shallots
4 garlic cloves
a few sprigs of thyme, basil or
    oregano

1 teaspoon sugar
1 teaspoon salt
½ teaspoon freshly
    ground black pepper
3 tablespoons olive oil

Preheat the oven to 180°C (350°F) gas mark 4.

Halve the tomatoes and spread in a single layer, cut side up, in a roasting tin. Peel and slice the shallots and garlic and scatter over the tomatoes with a few sprigs of thyme, basil or oregano. Sprinkle with the sugar, salt and pepper. Drizzle with the olive oil. Roast for 1 hour or until soft.

Rub the tomatoes through a nylon sieve or a mouli. Put in a saucepan, bring to the boil and pour into sterilised jars. Seal the jars. If using screw bands, release the lid by a quarter-turn. Put the jars in a saucepan with a folded cloth on the bottom, cover with warm water and bring slowly to simmering point over a period of 25 minutes. Simmer for 10 minutes. Remove the jars and stand them on a wooden base or folded tea towel. Tighten the screw bands if using. When cold, check the seal. Use within 12 months. Once opened, refrigerate and use within a few days.

This recipe is based on one in *Preserves: River Cottage Handbook No. 2* by Pam Corbin.

HUGH'S GLUTNEY

Makes 3–4 x 500ml (17fl oz) jars

After the end of September any tomatoes still on your plants are unlikely to ripen. But that doesn't mean they'll be wasted. Green tomatoes are an excellent basic ingredient in chutney and can be combined with another seasonal superfluous vegetable, the courgette that got away. It's only too easy to overlook the one lurking under the huge, spreading leaves of a courgette plant until it has almost reached marrow proportions.

½ teaspoon each of cloves, black peppercorns and coriander seeds
small piece of muslin, roughly 10cm (4in) square
675g (1lb 8oz) green tomatoes
675g (1lb 8oz) overgrown courgettes or marrows, peeled if using marrows and diced in 1cm (½in) pieces
675g (1lb 8oz) cooking apples, peeled, cored and diced (windfalls are fine)
250g (9oz) onions, peeled and roughly chopped

250g (9oz) sultanas or raisins
250g (9oz) light brown sugar
375ml (13fl oz) white wine or cider vinegar
200ml (7fl oz) water
1–2 teaspoons dried chilli flakes, depending on your taste for heat
½ teaspoon salt
½ teaspoon ground ginger

Prepare a spice bag by tying the cloves, peppercorns and coriander seeds into a square of muslin.

To peel the tomatoes, pour boiling water over them and leave for 1 minute. Remove with a slotted spoon and plunge into cold water. After 30 seconds, the skins will slip off easily. Chop the tomatoes and place them with the rest of the ingredients in a large, heavy pan.

Push the spice bag into the middle of the pan. Heat gently, stirring occasionally to dissolve the sugar. Bring to the boil, then simmer on a low heat for 1 hour, stirring regularly to stop it burning.

The chutney's ready when it is rich, thick and reduced, and parts to reveal the base of the pan when a wooden spoon is dragged through it. If it starts to dry out before this stage, add a little boiling water.

Place in sterilised jars with plastic-coated screw top lids while still warm, but not boiling hot.

From *The River Cottage Cookbook* by Hugh Fearnley-Whittingstall

All these methods of preserving food would have been familiar to wartime cooks. Their recipes for chutneys, pickles and jams were probably handed down within the family from generation to generation. They also salted runner and French beans in big glass jars or earthenware crocks.

From June 1941, the allocation of eggs was one per person a week. During the winter months when hens lay fewer eggs, this went down to one every two weeks. Town-dwellers lucky enough to have family or friends in the country would bring a dozen eggs back from a visit, if they could. Sometimes holiday makers and day trippers were able to buy eggs at the farm gate, and even in towns, neighbours with back garden hens might have a surplus to barter, or simply to give as a friendly gesture.

With eggs available from these sources it was worth putting down a few for later consumption. My mother did this. She kept a large earthenware bucket-shaped vessel with a lid, in the passage outside our kitchen, next to the mangle. The crock was full of isinglass, or 'water glass'. It looked like whitish, cloudy water, but was quite dense with a gelatinous texture that I found unpleasant to touch. I have since discovered it was made from the swim bladders of fishes. When we brought eggs home from my grandparents' farm, we carefully lowered them into the slimy gunge, layer upon layer. Isinglass preserves eggs by coating the shells to exclude all air, but you couldn't entirely trust it to keep every egg fresh. When you took one from the isinglass to cook with, you would break it into a cup to test it before adding it to the cake or pancake mixture. If it had gone off, you knew at once, from the sulphurous smell.

Jams and jellies played an important part in wartime food. Each person's ration of meat, butter and cheese was meagre, and bread was a valuable filler of hungry tummies. At teatime a doorstep slice spread thinly with marge was transformed into a treat by a generous layer of damson jam or bramble jelly.

The importance of jam was recognised by the Ministry of Food and extra rations of sugar were issued for jam making at the appropriate time of year. With this in mind, families would save up empty jam jars all the year round, queue at the greengrocer's to buy fruit when it was at its cheapest, and pick as many blackberries, crab apples and wild plums as they were able. Their reward was seeing rows of jars on the shelf, glowing like jewels and each neatly labelled with the fruit and the date, and crowned with a paper cap.

MINISTRY OF FOOD · LEAFLET · No. 10

Pickles and Chutney

GOOSEBERRY JAM

Makes 5–6 jars

There are few more satisfying kitchen occupations than jam making. Besides empty jars you need a pan large enough to be not more than half full when the fruit and sugar are in it, to avoid all risk of boiling over. Some fruits set as jam more easily than others because they contain more pectin. Pectin can be added in the form of apples or lemons, but the two examples I have chosen are high in pectin.

1kg (2lb 4oz) gooseberries
500ml (17fl oz) water
1kg (2lb 4oz) sugar

Using small scissors, top and tail the gooseberries. Put them in a pan with the water. Bring to the boil and simmer gently until the gooseberries are soft but still whole.

Add the sugar and stir until dissolved, taking care not to break the fruit. Bring to the boil and boil for 9–10 minutes.

Test for setting by dropping a little jam onto a cold saucer. Allow to cool a little then push it with your finger. If it crinkles, setting point has been reached. When set, remove from the heat and leave for 10 minutes.

Ladle into sterilised jam jars and, while still hot, cover each jar with a waxed disc then either a cellophane cover with a rubber band, or a screw top.

Variation: Replace a little of the sugar with elderflower syrup

RED CURRANT JELLY

Makes 4–5 jars

This is the classic accompaniment to Roast Lamb and main ingredient of Cumberland Sauce to serve with hot ham. Also good added to gravy to serve with game; to eat with cream cheese and goat's cheese; and for glazing fruit tarts.

I kg (2lb 4oz) red currants
400ml (14fl oz) water
sugar

Wash the red currants and put them, stalks and all, in a pan with the water. Simmer for about 45 minutes or until they are soft and have released all their juices.

Strain, preferably overnight, through a jelly bag or through a sheet of muslin tied at the corners to the legs of an up-ended chair. Do not push or squeeze the pulp through the filter or the jelly will be cloudy.

Measure the juice and put in a clean pan. Bring it to the boil and when boiling add 450g (1lb) sugar for every 600ml (21fl oz) juice. Stir until dissolved then boil hard for about 8 minutes until setting point is reached.

Test for setting by dropping a little jelly onto a cold saucer. Allow to cool a little, then push it with your finger. If it crinkles, setting point has been reached. When set, remove from the heat and leave for 10 minutes.

Ladle into sterilised jam jars and, while still hot, cover each jar with a waxed disc then either a cellophane cover with a rubber band, or a screw top.

Other jellies: Bramble jelly made with blackberries and apples; crab apple; quince; rowan.

Victory in the Garden

It was not long before the whole nation, it seemed, including King George VI and Queen Elizabeth, became involved in Digging for Victory. At Buckingham Palace a substantial area of the 40-acre garden was set aside for growing vegetables. Windsor Great Park became the largest wheat field in Britain and the Royal Parks in London were converted for food production. Allotments were provided in Kensington Gardens for Londoners, and a pig farm was established in Hyde Park. Even the (dry) moat at the Tower of London was dug up for allotments.

Seventy years on, royalty are again setting an example. For the first time since the War, vegetables are being grown in the garden of Buckingham Palace. Queen Elizabeth II's new vegetable plot measures just 40sq m (430sq ft) but there is plenty of room for expansion. Across the Atlantic, at 102sq m (1098sq ft), President and Mrs Obama's vegetable patch on the White House lawn is more than double the size of the Queen's. Even in the modest-sized garden at No. 10 Downing Street, the Prime Minister is setting a good example with a few raised vegetable beds.

The original Dig for Victory plan catered for an average allotment or back garden to measure, as it quaintly described it, 'approx 10 sq. rods, poles or perches.' This translates as 250sq m (2700sq ft), a formidable area to cultivate and care for. You could fit two White House plots into a 1940s Dig for Victory allotment and still have space for a Queen-sized plot beside them.

THE KNOWLEDGE

The organisers of Dig for Victory, aware that sound advice, especially to first-time vegetable gardeners, was crucial to the campaign's success, put together a travelling Dig for Victory Exhibition. Diarist Pam Ashford visited the exhibition in Glasgow and described it as 'small but nicely got up'. There were diagrams illustrating how to grow potatoes, tomatoes, turnips, parsnips, peas, beans, beetroots and fruit, advice on different ways to destroy insects, and suggestions for ensuring a supply of vegetables in winter as well as summer. She was particularly impressed by an exhibit of various bottled fruits, including one magnificent bottle containing 24 peaches.

Free Dig for Victory leaflets issued by the Ministry of Agriculture were a valuable source of information for allotment holders and gardeners and the advice in all 23 leaflets is still applicable and clearly expressed. Some dealt with the basics, such as *How to Dig, How to Sow Seeds* and *Pests and How to Deal with Them*. Other leaflets gave guidance on growing particular vegetables, such as No. 4, *Peas and Beans,* and No. 8 *Tomato Growing.* See Section 3 for practical month-by-month advice on what you should be doing in the garden.

Today's gardeners rely on TV gurus for how-to demonstrations, backed up with information from the books they publish. Britain's very first celebrity gardener was C.H. Middleton. His radio broadcasts, *In Your Garden* began in 1931, before the days of television. During the war some 3.5 million listeners would tune in to the BBC Home Service every Sunday afternoon to hear his horticultural tips. Mr Middleton, as he was always known, was a key figure in the Dig for Victory campaign, publicising it in his broadcasts. In 1942 he published a book, *Digging for Victory,* based on his broadcasts. In his introduction he wrote, 'These are critical times, but we shall get through them, and the harder we dig for victory the sooner will the roses be with us.'

Mr Middleton's style is avuncular, chatty and reassuring, and his advice is as useful now as it was in the 1930s and 1940s.

MORALE BOOSTERS

The government encouraged people to continue setting aside part of their garden for growing flowers, partly to keep up their morale and partly to ensure that there would still be a supply of seeds of ornamental plants when the war ended.

In one of his radio talks Mr Middleton suggested making a miniature flower garden with very little trouble or expense by sowing annuals such as marigolds, cornflowers, scarlet flax, coreopsis, godetias, nigella, and viscarias.

'You merely sow the seeds broadcast in groups or patches, rake them into the soil, and put a few short twigs among them to keep them upright... Or you might wait a bit and buy a box or two of dwarf antirrhinums, asters, stocks or lobelias. You can even plant them in the rockery if there are any bare spaces, and you can't afford new alpine plants. A bit unorthodox, perhaps, but what does that matter in wartime? What we are after is a few bright, cheerful flowers about the place.' (*Digging for Victory* by C.H. Middleton).

He also described another morale booster, important to the Dig for Victory campaign: the local village horticultural show. It was, he said in his broadcast in early September, an important event, giving people a day off from Hitler, reminding them of the good old days and enabling a nice little contribution to be sent to the Red Cross.

The show was held in the grounds of the local mansion, 'complete with flags, jangles and wangles, a band, a few speeches, darts competitions, bowling for a pig and other sideshows. There were classes for cookery and preserving, to encourage people to make the most of available food resources.

Some members of the many newly formed horticultural and allotment holders' societies questioned the wisdom of holding a show at a time of petrol restrictions and difficulty in providing refreshments. Would members' time not be better employed in their gardens or on their allotments? Mr Middleton came down firmly on the other side of the argument. 'There will always be local Jeremiahs to throw cold water on every suggestion,' he said, 'but

don't heed them.' The show, he felt, was the climax of a successful season, the gathering of the clans, the great day of reckoning when members can compare results, enter into friendly arguments, and show each other what they can really do.

Gardeners love to swank a bit, he said, and the show brings them together in a pleasant, albeit competitive atmosphere. The prizes might be 'a nice set of carvers, although I don't know what I'm going to carve with them if I get them,' said Mr Middleton, 'or perhaps a tin of fertiliser or a gardening book, or half a crown [2 shillings and sixpence], so I go out every morning and look at the onions and measure the runner beans, and see if the tomatoes are colouring up... There is something extremely satisfying about winning a prize at a show.'

GROWING UP – THE VERTICAL GARDEN

Standard 300sq yard (249sq m) allotments could, according to a Ministry of Information Dig for Victory film, produce enough vegetables to feed a family of five for eight months of the year. It would need tending, the film optimistically stated, for an hour or two a week – so much more rewarding than an hour or two spent queuing at the greengrocer's.

You would have to be very dedicated to cultivate a full-sized allotment, even with the enthusiastic help of the rest of the family, and many plots are, and were, officially divided into halves, or, by informal arrangement, shared by more than one family.

The back garden of an average terraced house is a great deal smaller,

USE SPADES NOT SHIPS

GROW YOUR OWN FOOD

AND SUPPLY YOUR OWN COOKHOUSE

cumbers can all be trained on trellises, wigwams or horizontal wires stretched between two posts. Galvanised pig wire, with its wide square mesh, makes an excellent support for climbing plants if it is firmly fixed to a wall or to stout posts. Roofs and balconies on upper floors are often exposed to high winds, so if it's not possible to fix trellis or wire to the walls of the building, plant posts into flowerpots and fill the pots with concrete to make a sturdy base.

Some plants will happily trail downwards: dwarf or bush beans, as opposed to climbing varieties; strawberries; 'Little Marvell' peas; and trailing tomatoes like 'Tumbler' and 'Tumbling Tom' can be planted among the climbers, at the edges of the container.

WE DIG THE GROUND AND SCATTER

Dig for Victory leaflets and films showed people how to dig, sow seeds and carry out other basic gardening techniques. If you have never dug over a plot of ground, or have only dug a small area, you may wonder what all the fuss is about. Surely, the first-timer thinks, you just stick the spade in the ground, lift it out with a clod of earth on it, turn the clod over and drop it. But there is a right way and a wrong way, and the difference will be felt in your back and shoulders. Many professional gardeners have spent a lifetime using the wrong digging technique, and that is why they walk around bent double.

For beginners, and as a refresher for old hands, here are updated instructions for the basics:

but still offers potential for grow-your-own gardening. To make the best use of all available space, the Ministry of Information's film suggested growing vegetables on top of the corrugated steel Anderson air raid shelters that many families installed in their back gardens. It also showed a woman industriously hoeing a row of lettuces on a flat roof. No yard, flat roof or balcony is too small for a group of tubs, troughs and pots. Even a window box provides growing space. The only problems are likely to be getting compost to the pots and providing a regular water supply.

Where space is at a premium, it makes sense to make full use of the vertical dimension. Peas, beans (French and runner), squashes, tomatoes and cu-

DIGGING

WHY? Digging breaks up compacted soil so that the roots of plants can penetrate, worms and other soil-improving creatures can do their work and drainage is improved. It lets in air to speed the breakdown of organic matter, making more nutrients available to plants. Digging provides an opportunity to add manure, compost and other soil improvers.

Digging a plot

1. To dig a rectangular area, start by digging a trench along the shorter side, removing the soil in a wheelbarrow and depositing it at the other end of the plot.

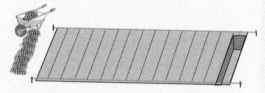

2. At this stage you can, if needed, spread organic material or fertiliser at the bottom of the trench. Dig along the face of the trench, turning the soil into the trench, thus forming a new trench parallel to the first.

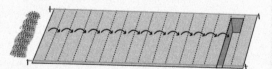

3. Continue digging until you reach the end of the plot. Fill the final trench with the soil from the first.

WHEN? Let nature do the job, particularly if your soil is heavy clay. In autumn and early winter, turn the soil over roughly. Frost, wind, snow and rain will break the clods down during the winter. When spring comes, all you need do is break up remaining lumps by bashing them with a fork. Choose a day when the soil is easy to work. If it is too wet, it will stick to your boots and your spade, and lifting a spadeful will be hard on your back and shoulder muscles. Digging and standing on wet soil causes compaction, which can damage the soil structure.

HOW? Correct digging is a three-stage technique, using your body weight rather than your muscles. Work 'backwards'; so you are not treading on dug soil.

1. Cutting the soil: keep the spade vertical and drive it into the soil by leaning on it from above, with one foot on top of the spade. Don't push it in with your arms and shoulders.

2. Lifting the soil: pull the spade handle towards you and lean on it to lever up a spadeful of soil, bending your knees.

3. Turning the soil: straighten your knees, twisting the spade to one side to turn the soil over as you drop it.

When buying a spade, choose one which feels right for you. It should not be too heavy and should have a long enough shaft. Too short a spade shaft is a frequent cause of back problems.

Take small spadefuls and stop before you feel tired; to begin with 30 minutes is probably long enough. Stop and do something else using different muscles before you go back to your digging.

LEVELLING

Before you sow seeds you need to break down any clods and level out lumps and bumps.

WHEN? In spring or at any other time when you are going to sow seeds. Choose a day when the soil is dry on top but moist underneath.

We must still make the best use of garden or allotment to produce supplies of home-grown food. This leaflet helps you to grow more vegetables, and shows you how to turn them into health-giving dishes.

**GARDEN HINTS
BY THE MINISTRY OF AGRICULTURE**

RECIPES
BY THE MINISTRY OF FOOD
MARCH TO APRIL ISSUE

HOW? Using a metal rake, stand upright and push the rake back and forth in front of you, using long strokes and moving backwards in a straight line.

The technique is to push away harder than you pull towards you, and not to lean on the rake as that will cause the tines to dig in and will interrupt your rhythm.

At the end of each line you will have raked up a small pile of stones, twigs and other debris. Remove them into a bucket.

When you have raked over the plot in one direction, rake it again at a right angle.

THE NO-DIG GARDEN

Who wants to dig if they don't have to? The theory is that, after thorough initial preparation of the ground, you sit back and let the worms do the work. They aerate the soil as they move through it and convert organic matter into humus as it moves through them. The beds need only be mulched with compost or well-rotted farmyard manure each year. Because digging often causes dormant weed seeds to germinate, the no-dig system should almost eliminate weeds after a few years. The soil will be of such good structure and open texture that those weeds that do appear will be easy to remove. The soil also builds up a high level of fertility so that plants can be grown closer together, leaving no room for weeds.

For the system to succeed you must avoid compacting the soil by walking on it, especially in wet conditions. Beds should be no wider than 1.2–1.5m (4–5ft) so that you can reach the centre from either side. The no-dig system works very well on raised beds where the soil is held 24–48cm (2–4ft) above the level of the paths. The drainage is better and the soil warms up quicker in spring.

MAKING RAISED BEDS

As an alternative to growing vegetables in long, narrow rows with space to walk between the rows, many people prefer a system of raised beds with permanent pathways between them, especially where space is limited. The beds can be contained by wood, brick or even stacked turf. The paths between them can be flagstones, concrete, gravel, mown grass or just trodden earth.

Raised beds can be anything between 45–120cm (18in–4ft) above ground level. They should be narrow enough for the gardener to be able to reach the centre from the path; between 90cm and 120cm (3–4ft) The length of the beds can be adapted to suit the shape and size of the plot and the paths should be wide enough to accommodate a wheelbarrow.

WHY? Drainage is improved and the soil warms up quicker in the spring. You avoid compacting the soil by walking on it. Some crops do better when planted in rectangular blocks rather than in lines.

HOW? You will need: four 2 x 6in (5 x 20 cm) boards of the correct length, four 4 x 4's of 40cm in length, sharpened at one end, and 3½in nails or 3in screws.

SOWING SEEDS

WHEN? Follow the instructions on the seed packet, and see under individual crops below. In general, sow tender or half-hardy plants such as climbing beans, French beans, courgettes, tomatoes and sweetcorn in early spring. Hardy crops can be sown outdoors at intervals so that they mature in succession. Sow the first lot

Making Raised Beds

1. Assemble two sides of the frame first. Carefully line up the edges of one of the planks and two of the stakes and nail or screw the plank securely to the stake. Pre-drilling the holes will prevent the wood from splitting.

2. Nail one of the free planks onto other side of the stake. Continue around the square by attaching the other assembled section.

3. Nail the remaining plank onto the structure and it's finished. Once in position, carefully hammer the stakes into the ground using a mallet.

in spring after the soil has warmed up, on a day when the soil is moist but not wet.

WHERE? Sow tender or half-hardy plants in trays or individual pots of all-purpose compost in the greenhouse or on a windowsill. Hardy plants can be started off in the greenhouse for an earlier crop, or sown straight into the ground, observing your chosen crop rotation system (see below).

Sowing seeds

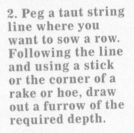

1. Rake the soil to a fine tilth, the texture of breadcrumbs.

2. Peg a taut string line where you want to sow a row. Following the line and using a stick or the corner of a rake or hoe, draw out a furrow of the required depth.

3. Sprinkle the seeds thinly and evenly along the furrow or place large individual seeds (e.g. peas, beans) the required distance apart. With your foot push the soil gently back over the seeds and firm lightly. Label the row. Water thoroughly using a fine rose.

CROP ROTATION

The best way to grow vegetables is to divide your plot into sections so that you can observe a rotation of crops. This means you don't grow the same crop in the same place two years running, so soil-borne diseases don't have a chance to build up. You can also provide each category of crop with the conditions it prefers.

Dig For Victory Leaflet No. 1 showed coloured illustrations of a detailed cropping plan, designed for a 10-rod plot. For those without access to such a large garden, there was also a cropping plan for a plot half that size, 45 x 30ft (13 ³/₄ x 9m). The cropping plan is still a sensible model to follow, it is planned for a 2-year rotation, but vegetables fall more naturally into three groups, and a three-year rotation is just as easy to follow in a small space as in a large one.

The main Dig for Victory cropping plan is designed for a three-year rotation, with the main vegetable crops divide into three categories. So you need three plots. But you will also want to grow some more permanent plants outside the rotation: globe artichokes, perhaps, and rhubarb; strawberries, raspberries, gooseberries and currants; if your garden is large enough you may want an asparagus bed. So you need a fourth plot for these long-term plants. How much space this takes up depends on the size of your garden and your priorities. The other three plots should be roughly the same size as each other.

The three vegetable groups to rotate are as follows:

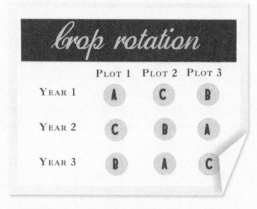

crop rotation

	PLOT 1	PLOT 2	PLOT 3
YEAR 1	A	C	B
YEAR 2	C	B	A
YEAR 3	B	A	C

A. POTATOES AND ROOTS
Carrots, parsnips, celery, celeriac, beetroot, salsify, spinach beet and seakale beet. Root vegetables don't like freshly manured ground as it can cause their roots to bifurcate and become distorted.

C. LEGUMES: PEAS AND BEANS
They thrive on soil to which manure or compost has been added. Legumes release nitrogen which particularly benefits leafy crops in group B.

B. BRASSICAS
Cabbage, cauliflower, Brussels sprouts, purple sprouting broccoli, calabrese, Pak choi, Chinese cabbages, swedes, turnips, spinach. They are nitrogen-hungry, so should follow after legumes.

There is a fourth group sometimes added into the equation to make a four-year rotation, consisting mainly of onions and other alliums, notably leeks. The Ministry of Food's 3-year rotation plan included them in the same group as legumes, and called that group 'miscellaneous crops'. Other miscellaneous vegetables that can be grown without

reference to the rotational plan include spinach, lettuce, rocket, spring onions, radishes and other salad greens. They can be sown between the rows of other crops, or follow on after earlier crops have been harvested.

WHAT TO GROW?
Within each group there is a wide choice of crops to grow, and, unless you are aiming for complete self-sufficiency in vegetables, you can be selective. During the war some crops, such as onions, potatoes, and virtually all winter vegetables, became very important and it was a patriotic duty to grow as much as possible of such everyday items. Things are different now, and some gardeners may not want the hassle of growing vegetables that are readily available in the shops at relatively low cost, particularly if they are short of space.

Onions, which had previously been imported from Brittany and the Channel Islands, completely disappeared from the shops early in the war, so growing your own became very worthwhile. Today, however, they are plentiful and cheap, and I defy anyone to tell the difference between a bought and a home-grown onion.

Leeks are a different matter. A leek freshly dug from the garden has a sweetness lacking in most bought leeks. They don't take up much space and can be popped into the ground to follow on after peas and broad beans have been harvested. In the list of vegetables that follows, reasons for growing them are included with advice on how to succeed with them.

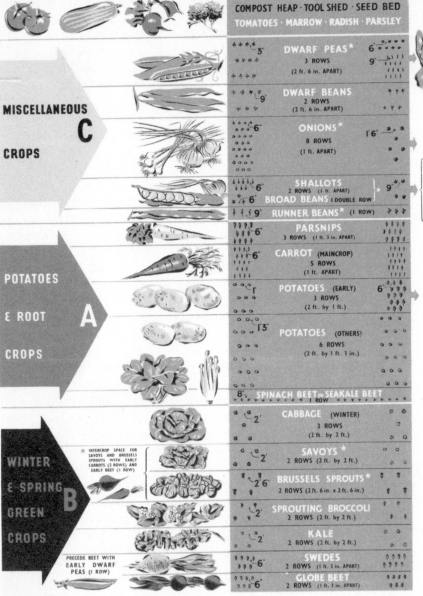

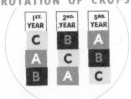

POTATO PETE

Potatoes, being something of a miracle food, were of paramount importance during the war. Before the war, bread and potatoes were the staple fillers of the British diet. Without them, poor families would have starved. But during the war the government wanted to discourage the consumption of bread because so much of the wheat flour to make it had to be imported. As we have seen, great efforts were made to meet the shortfall in imported flour by ploughing up grassland to grow wheat. But supplies were still low and the government's policy was to wean people off bread and encourage them to grow and eat potatoes instead.

The Ministry's policy gave birth to Potato Pete, a cartoon character who not only gave advice on growing and cooking potatoes, but also produced his own potato recipe books and inspired spud-promoting songs on radio and in the cinema. The songs proved popular although the lyrics were fairly basic:

'Potatoes new. Potatoes old
Potato (in a salad) cold
Potatoes baked or mashed or fried
Potatoes whole, potato pied
Enjoy them all including chips
Remembering spuds don't come in ships.'

Ministry of Food advertisement

Harry Roy and his band, a popular orchestra performing at smart clubs and restaurants, added the Potato Pete Foxtrot to a repertoire that included 'She Had to Go and Lose it at the Astor' and 'Top Hat, White Tie and Tails'.

The Ministry of Food offered a weekly prize to the greengrocer with the best

POTATOES
feed without fattening and give you *ENERGY*

potato display, and organised an event called Potato Pete's Fair in Oxford Street, London. Visitors to the fair could buy 'Potato Stamps' to exchange for extra potatoes at their greengrocer.

Out of 23 leaflets issued by the Ministry of Agriculture to gardeners and allotment holders, four were devoted to the subject: Seed Potatoes, Storing Potatoes, Potato Growing and, rather depressingly, Potato Blight. Nowadays the 'can't tell the difference between home grown and bought' rule applies, except in the case of new potatoes such as Foremost and Dunluce, and a few varieties of main-crop which have the same waxy flesh as new potatoes, notably Ratte and Pink Fir Apple. When the time taken for them to travel from garden to pot to plate is only a matter of hours, they have an earthy depth of flavour that no bought potato can supply.

Potato Pete's recipe book

GROWING POTATOES

WHERE? In an open, sunny site, not in a frost pocket. Choose good soil, preferably slightly acid, but potatoes tolerate neutral and alkaline soil. Dig in some well-rotted manure or compost.

WHEN? Chit the potatoes (see 'how?' below) in February, about six weeks before planting. Remember to order your seed potatoes early to make sure they arrive in good time. Plant them out in spring when there is less risk of heavy frost and the ground has started to warm up. This depends on your local climate, but usually about the end of March.

HOW? See Growing Potatoes diagram below. Chitting (waiting for the seed potatoes to put out new shoots) is essen-tial before planting. Each seed potato has a more rounded, blunt end with a number of 'eyes' that will develop into shoots.

HARVEST When flower buds appear on the stems above ground, gently loosen the earth around a plant using a fork, so you can inspect the little potatoes. It's up to you when to harvest them. The bigger they get the less waxy and more floury the texture becomes. Early potatoes are 'new' potatoes, and should be dug and eaten when still quite small. Main-crop mature later than earlies and some varieties can be stored for winter use.

TIP: Extend the harvesting season by sowing rows at intervals of 2 weeks.

Growing POTATOES

1. Stand the tubers with the blunt end uppermost in shallow trays or egg boxes, and place them in a light, frost-free place. A north-facing window sill in an unheated room or shed is ideal. When the shoots are about 2cm (3/4in) long they are ready to plant.

2. Dig a trench 71/2–15cm (3–6in) deep. Fork in manure or compost at the bottom of the trench. Place the seed potatoes gently into the trench, taking care not to break off the shoots. Plant earlies 30cm (12in) apart with 40–50cm (16–20in) between the rows. Plant main-crop potatoes 38cm (15in) apart with 75cm (30in) between rows. Cover them lightly with soil.

3. When the shoots appear, rake up the soil from each side to just bury them, making a long ridge along the row. This is known as 'earthing up'. Do this at regular intervals until the ridge is about 15cm (6in) high. New potatoes may be ready from June onward.

DOCTOR CARROT
the Children's best friend

DR CARROT

Potato Pete was sometimes to be seen more or less hand-in-hand with a character called Dr Carrot in the pages of women's magazines and on recipe leaflets.

Although the Ministry focussed on getting people to buy carrots rather than to grow them, Mr Middleton, in one of his April 'Digging for Victory' broadcasts, encouraged gardeners to sow carrots as a summer treat: 'In the winter we eat them as a sort of national duty, whether we like them or not, but in the summer we eat them for pleasure, for of all the early vegetables, there is surely none sweeter than a dish of fresh young carrots, unless it be the first green peas, and the two go very well together, and help to make life worth living, even now.'

His advice was to grow stump-rooted varieties, and not to thin them out as this 'attracts the fly; she smells them so much easier when they have been disturbed, and then comes and lays her eggs in the holes left by the thinning.' Mr Middleton fed his carrots on a mixture of fine bone meal and dried blood fertiliser sprinkled thinly on the ground from an old sugar dredger, then raked in. His method works just as well for the long varieties.

GROWING CARROTS

WHERE? In well broken up ground that was manured for another crop the previous year. They do well in the loose soil of raised beds, but struggle in heavy clay soils.

WHEN? Starting in spring, sow early carrots once a fortnight, and repeat for up to three months. Sow main-crop varieties to store for winter at the end of May or first week in June.

HOW?
1. If not already done, fork over the ground, breaking up lumps and removing stones. Either make a drill at least 5cm (2in) wide and 1cm (½in) deep with a hoe, or rake a rectangular area to a fine tilth.
2. Sow the carrot seeds very sparingly.
3. Cover them with 1cm (½in) fine soil.
4. Tread gently to firm the soil.
5. Water with a fine spray if necessary.
6. Continue to water in dry spells.

Protect from carrot root fly using a protective barrier of fine mesh netting or clear plastic 30–60cm (2–3ft) high. This is easier to install if the carrots are sown in a rectangular block rather than a long row.

HARVEST Early varieties are ready after 7–9 weeks, main-crop 10–11 weeks. Pull them up or lift them with a fork, thinning as you go. Break off the green tops and remove them to the compost heap. Don't leave them on site as the smell attracts carrot flies.

Main-crop carrots keep their sweetness and crunchiness all winter if stored as follows:

CARROTS
keep you healthy and help you to see in the blackout

1. Dig up the roots at any time from October to December. Cut off the leaves 1cm (½in) from the root.
2. Place 1cm (½in) of sand or newspaper in the bottom of a wooden or cardboard box.
3. Put a single layer of carrots on it, not touching each other. Cover with another 1cm (½in) of insulation, then place another layer of carrots in the box, then a layer of sand or paper. Continue until the box is full.
4. Store in a dry, frost-free place and protect from mice.

Carrots can also be diced or sliced and frozen for use in soups and stews.

THE REST OF THE ROOTS

The Ministry did not see fit to anthropomorphise other vegetables in Group A, so there is no Bertie Beetroot, Professor Parsnip or Tommy Turnip. But they were useful ingredients in soups and stews, and played an essential part by filling the hungry winter gap when other vegetables were not available. Personally, I would have added celeriac to the list, but it doesn't seem to feature often in wartime recipes, or in the wartime vegetable garden. It has the advantage of being just as good raw (grated with a mustardy mayonnaise dressing) as it is cooked (delicious thinly sliced in a gratin), which you can't say for beetroots, parsnips, swedes and turnips.

For cultivation and winter storage of all these roots, the method is similar to that described above for carrots. But as they are all readily available throughout the winter in greengrocers, farmers' markets and supermarkets, they are only worth growing if you have plenty of space, or if you prefer your beetroots and turnips the size of ping pong balls rather than tennis balls. The smaller they are, the more tender they are too.

LEGUMES

'Peas and beans are valuable garden crops. As both green and dried seeds, they constitute the most nutritious of all vegetables. They contain flesh building and energizing elements, and they should therefore occupy an important place in the family garden.' Dig for Victory leaflet No. 4

These are the plants that fix nitrogen in the soil by means of nodules on their roots. When you have harvested the crop, instead of digging up the plants, cut them down to the ground, but leave the roots to complete their work, so that the greens that follow can have full benefit from the nitrogen.

GROWING PEAS

WHERE? In an open site, in fertile, moisture-retentive but well-drained soil. Avoid cold, wet soils and dry, sandy soils. Dig in plenty of well-rotted manure or compost during the autumn or winter before sowing.

WHEN? In spring. Wait until the soil has warmed up, then sow at 2-week intervals. Avoid sowing in mid-summer as high temperatures inhibit germination.

HOW?

1. Using a draw hoe, make out a flat-bottomed drill about 15cm (6in) wide and 3cm (1¼in) deep.

2. Sow the seeds 5cm (2in) apart in both directions. Cover with soil and firm gently with your foot.

3. When the young shoots develop tendrils, fix up supports, 1.2m (4ft) high or more, according to the variety you are growing. Use traditional pea sticks (twiggy hazel branches) or netting (wire or plastic) fixed to canes.

4. At the same time, mulch the peas with 5cm (2in) well-rotted compost. this will help to retain moisture and keep the roots cool.

5. Water regularly during dry spells, when the plants are in flower and pods are forming.

HARVEST Pick the peas as they become ready. Raw peas, picked, shelled and eaten on the spot are hard to resist.

It's not worth growing peas in order to freeze them, as excellent frozen peas can be bought, but if you happen to have a surplus, freezing them takes very little time.

GROWING BROAD BEANS (FAVA BEANS)

WHERE? In the same plot as other legumes (peas and other beans).

WHEN? For an early crop, sow in late autumn to early winter the year before. Otherwise sow from early spring to early summer, or sow in pots indoors in late winter to plant out in spring.

HOW?
1. Sow them in double rows with 90cm (3ft) between the double rows or in blocks, with the seeds 23cm (9in) apart and 4cm (1½ in) deep.
2. In windy areas support the plants with wire attached to posts outside the rows or around the blocks.
2. Water when flower buds appear if the weather is dry.
3. When the plants are in flower nip off the growing tips to remove black-fly and encourage pods to form.

HARVEST The growing tips and very young pods can be cooked and eaten. Otherwise pick and shell when the beans are about the size of a fingernail.

Broad beans freeze very well, retaining their flavour and texture for at least a year. Baby broad beans from the freezer are a Christmas treat in our family.

GROWING CLIMBING BEANS (FRENCH AND RUNNERS)

'No vegetable crop responds to and repays kindly treatment better than the runner bean. You can get beans, of a sort, without much trouble, but if you want a good crop of good beans you've got to treat them generously.' *Digging for Victory* by C.H. Middleton.

WHERE? In a sheltered position in the same plot as other legumes, in ground with plenty of manure and/or compost dug in. Avoid frost pockets.

WHEN? French beans and runner beans are susceptible to frost, so wait until early summer when there is little danger of a frost and the soil has warmed up. Alternatively, sow them earlier in pots indoors or in a greenhouse.

HOW?
Using 2½ m (8ft) canes or traditional bean poles, make a wigwam of 4 canes/poles or a double row of canes/poles, crossed at the top and tied to

a horizontal cane. The rows of canes should be 60–90cm (2–3ft) apart, with the canes in each row 30–45cm (1–1½ft) apart.

Climbing beans are all attractive in leaf, flower and pod, so can also be effectively grown in the flower garden over arches, tunnels and pergolas.

1. Sow one bean at the foot of each pole, 4cm (1½in) deep.

2. The seedlings should soon take hold of the canes and climb up, but in a windy site they may initially need to be tied on with string.

3. Cut off the main stems when they reach the top of the supports.

4. Water during dry weather, preferably with a weak liquid manure.

HARVEST Start picking when the beans are young. The more you pick the more you get. When you get tired of eating French beans, leave them to grow bigger and shell the seeds when half-ripe (flageolets) and fully mature (haricots). This doesn't work for runners.

Runner beans freeze well and will keep for at least 3 months. French beans don't.

Warning: never eat French beans raw as they contain toxins that must be destroyed by cooking.

GROWING DWARF BEANS

Dwarf French beans make short, bushy plants and require the same growing conditions as climbers. Plant them 22cm (9in) apart in staggered rows for the best yield. Compared with other crops they give high yields in relatively small spaces, so are good to grow in pots and window boxes.

BRASSICAS

These are the plants that come after the legumes in the crop rotation, so that they can benefit from the nitrogen the peas and beans have provided. Mr Middleton said in one of his broadcasts, 'there's a lot to be said for a good cabbage, especially when you haven't got one.' But today we have not only cabbages, but also calabrese, cauliflowers, kale and Brussels sprouts, and it's hard to tell the difference between home-grown and bought. Purple sprouting broccoli is different. Once cut, the sappy, snappy shoots quickly become flabby and the flavour goes off. It is probably the one brassica worth growing at home, for the shortest possible journey from plot to pot.

That's not to say that cabbage is not worth buying and eating – or even drinking:

'I'm feeling stronger than I have been for years... I think it is due to my "cabbage water", the drink I was told to take by the London doctor. It really is marvellous and one gets to like it. You should try it. You chop up cabbage small, grate carrot and put in plenty of parsley, also spinach or watercress if you like, bring to the boil, simmer 20 minutes, strain off and add marmite to taste. Drink two or three glasses a day. It's a marvellous tonic and full of vitamins' (Miss W. Ransford, 24th November 1941).

GROWING PURPLE SPROUTING BROCCOLI

WHERE? On ground used the previous year for peas and beans. Choose a sheltered spot and avoid poor, sandy soil.

WHEN? Sow the seeds in March to May. Plant out young plants in early to mid summer.

HOW?

1. Sow thinly outdoors in a seed bed, or indoors in trays or pots of moist compost, about 4 seeds to a 9cm (3½in) pot. Water in dry spells. Plant out in final positions, at least 60cm (2ft) apart, planting firmly and deeply, about 15cm (6in) for stability.

2. When the plants are 45cm (18in) high, stake each one with a 1¼m (4ft) cane.

3. Erect a cage of plastic netting around the broccoli plants to protect them from marauding pigeons. Don't worry if the caterpillars of Cabbage White butterflies make lace of the leaves; this will not prevent the young shoots sprouting in March.

HARVEST Pick the shoots from early spring when they are about 15cm (6in) long and the flower buds are still tightly closed. For the next 2 months the more you pick the more will grow.

MISCELLANEOUS CROPS

These don't fit into the 3-year crop rotation plan, but you wouldn't want to be without them. Tomatoes and courgettes can both produce prolific crops and (a bonus for the cook, this) need no peeling or cleaning. Salad crops grow so quickly that they can be tucked into the vegetable plot wherever there is a space.

TOMATOES

Given a good, warm summer, tomatoes planted in a sunny, sheltered spot, will thrive and ripen well, but if you have space in a greenhouse, you will get earlier and more reliable results. At the end of the season green tomatoes can sometimes be induced to ripen:

‘There are several ways of ripening green tomatoes; some put them between layers of flannel in a box – my mother al-

Growing TOMATOES

1. Transplant indoor seedlings into 6cm (3in) pots when 3 leaves have developed. Transplant potted seedlings into pots or grow bags, 45cm (1½ ft) apart.

2. Support upright varieties by tying the main stems to canes as they grow. Bush types don't need support.

3. Pinch outside shoots on upright varieties as they grow, so that the plant's energy goes into forming fruit. Feed plants in grow bags or pots regularly using a proprietary liquid tomato food. Follow the instructions on the bottle. Water outdoor plants in dry spells.

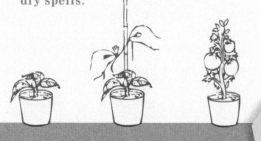

ways did that, and put them in a dark cupboard, and she used to make them last nearly up to Christmas; some pack them in sawdust or put them on shelves in the greenhouse, or along the window ledge, and they all claim theirs to be the best and only way to do it. Actually, I don't think it matters much – warmth is the most important factor; if a tomato has passed a certain stage it will finish the ripening process in any warm corner, light or dark. I really believe they do it better in the dark though I shouldn't like to explain why.' (Mr Middleton, broadcasting in September).

GROWING TOMATOES

WHERE? The sunniest, most sheltered spot you can find, with plenty of well-rotted manure dug in; or in a greenhouse.

WHEN? Sow the seeds indoors in early spring or outside in late spring. Plant young plants outdoors when all risk of frost is gone.

HOW? Sow seeds in situ outdoors or in seed trays inside. Thin out outdoor seedlings to 45cm (1½ ft) apart.

HARVEST Start picking as soon as the tomatoes ripen, and keep picking until they stop ripening. Green tomatoes can be used to make chutney (see page 46). If you have a glut, make passata and bottle it (see page 45).

COURGETTES

Courgettes (or zucchini) didn't feature in gardening advice or recipe books during the war. In those days size seemed to matter and British gardeners and cooks valued vegetable marrows of prize-winning dimensions. Marrows were recommended to grow on top of Anderson shelters, the back garden bomb shelters, which were half-buried and had a 38cm (15in) layer of soil on their roofs. It was said that you were more likely to be injured by a marrow falling on your head than by a bomb.

I have unhappy childhood memories of watery and fibrous lumps of marrow served in white sauce, but stuffed marrow can be good if the marrow is no bigger than an overgrown courgette. Recipes for marrow and ginger jam appear in wartime cookery books and a *Daily Telegraph* book of readers' recipes offers Marrow Compote, and Junket.

It seems safer to prevent courgettes from growing into marrows (the opposite of ugly ducklings and swans). Each plant will yield as much, since the more you pick, the more fruit you get.

GROWING COURGETTES

WHERE? In an open, sunny place in well-drained but moisture-retentive soil enriched with well-rotted manure.

WHEN? Outdoors after all risk of frost has passed, or indoors in pots in spring.

HOW?
1. Sow the seeds 2.5cm (1in) deep and about 90cm (3ft) apart.
2. Mulch with 5cm (2in) compost after planting.
3. Water copiously in dry spells.

Plan and Grow for Winter

Planned crops for garden wealth

Assure the family's winter health

HARVEST Pick when 10cm (4in) long. The flowers can be stuffed, battered and deep-fried.

SALAD CROPS

Before, during and for some time after the war, the British idea of a salad was a few lettuce leaves, a tomato cut in half, a few slices of cucumber, a couple of radishes, a spring onion and a sprinkling of cress. The only variations were the addition of sliced beetroot or some grated carrot or, to convert it from a side dish into a main course, a hardboiled egg. Sometimes all three were included, the beetroot's life-blood seeping out to stain the egg and the carrot.

Today we can do a good deal better, and a wide selection of salad leaves is available to grow from seed. Lettuce, rocket and other leaves, radishes and spring onions, are all quick-growing and can be sown in short rows between other, slower crops. For spacings, follow the instructions on the seed packets.

HERBS

Frugal wartime dishes, such as meat-less vegetable pies and stews, cry out for extra flavouring, yet advice about herbs and spices is notably absent from most Second World War gardening and cookery books. The occasional recipe for parsley sauce or one including a teaspoon of mixed herbs and the instruction to 'sprinkle with a little chopped parsley before serving' is about as far as they go with herbs. As for spices, I have come across recipes for curried carrots, curried cod and curried corned beef balls. A spoonful or two of curry powder or paste is still not to be despised and gives a quick lift to a bland or tired dish.

For a modern take on thrifty food, no garden, balcony or windowsill should be without rosemary, bay, sage, thyme, chives, parsley and tarragon. Except for sage and parsley, these herbs all need a sunny spot, preferably close to the kitchen.

A well-planned ten rod garden yields These vegetables for winter meals.

* Ministry of Agricult

Lindum Hotel, St. An

WELL-PLANNED PLOT

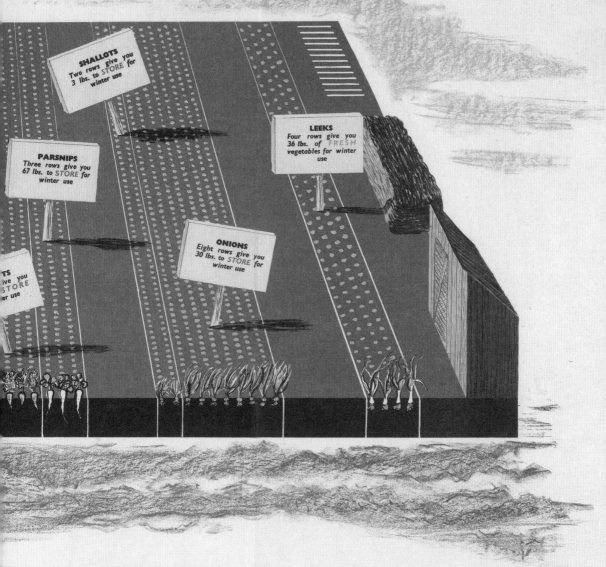

SHALLOTS
Two rows give you 3 lbs. to STORE for winter use

PARSNIPS
Three rows give you 67 lbs. to STORE for winter use

LEEKS
Four rows give you 36 lbs. of FRESH vegetables for winter use

ONIONS
Eight rows give you 30 lbs. to STORE for winter use

**The Cropping Plan tells how it's done:
Send to the M.A.F.* for one**

nd Fisheries,
n-Sea, Lancs.

THE KITCHEN FRONT

'Keep the home fires burning,
While your hearts are yearning,
Though your lads are far away
They dream of Home;
There's a silver lining
Through the dark cloud shining
Turn the dark cloud inside out,
Till the boys come home.'

First World War song: lyrics by Lena Guilbert Ford

Keeping the home fires burning was not much easier during the Second World War than it had been in the First. The sheer drudgery of domestic life is illustrated by Gwen Millard's description of her mother's life in Leamington Spa.

'How can I get across how hard she worked during the war? A house that contained her family, soldiers billeted on us, and evacuees. She and millions of housewives like her were the unsung heroes of the war... They wrote letters and sent parcels to the men and women away from home, and kept their families warm and fed as best they could. My mum kept a large house spotlessly clean, and all without electricity and running hot water. We had gas light... The gas copper in the kitchen did for the very large weekly wash, as well as to fill the bath in the kitchen. [There were no dishwashers, washing machines, or even launderettes.] We ironed with a gas iron that had a long metal flex that fitted onto a gas jet.

I used to turn the handle of the big mangle that stood in the larder, while my mother fed sheets and towels and other articles through it, after she had washed them by hand, or boiled them in the copper.

When the raids on Coventry were at their height there were nights when the sirens went and Mum didn't get a lot of sleep. I am ashamed to say now I took her for granted. She was my Mum and that's what mums did.'

Coming home from work, or from the shops, before putting the kettle on for tea the housewife might have to stoke up the kitchen range, bringing a bucket of coke fuel in from the coal hole to feed the damped down fire. Many homes still lacked gas and electricity, and very few had central heating, so keeping warm in winter was a

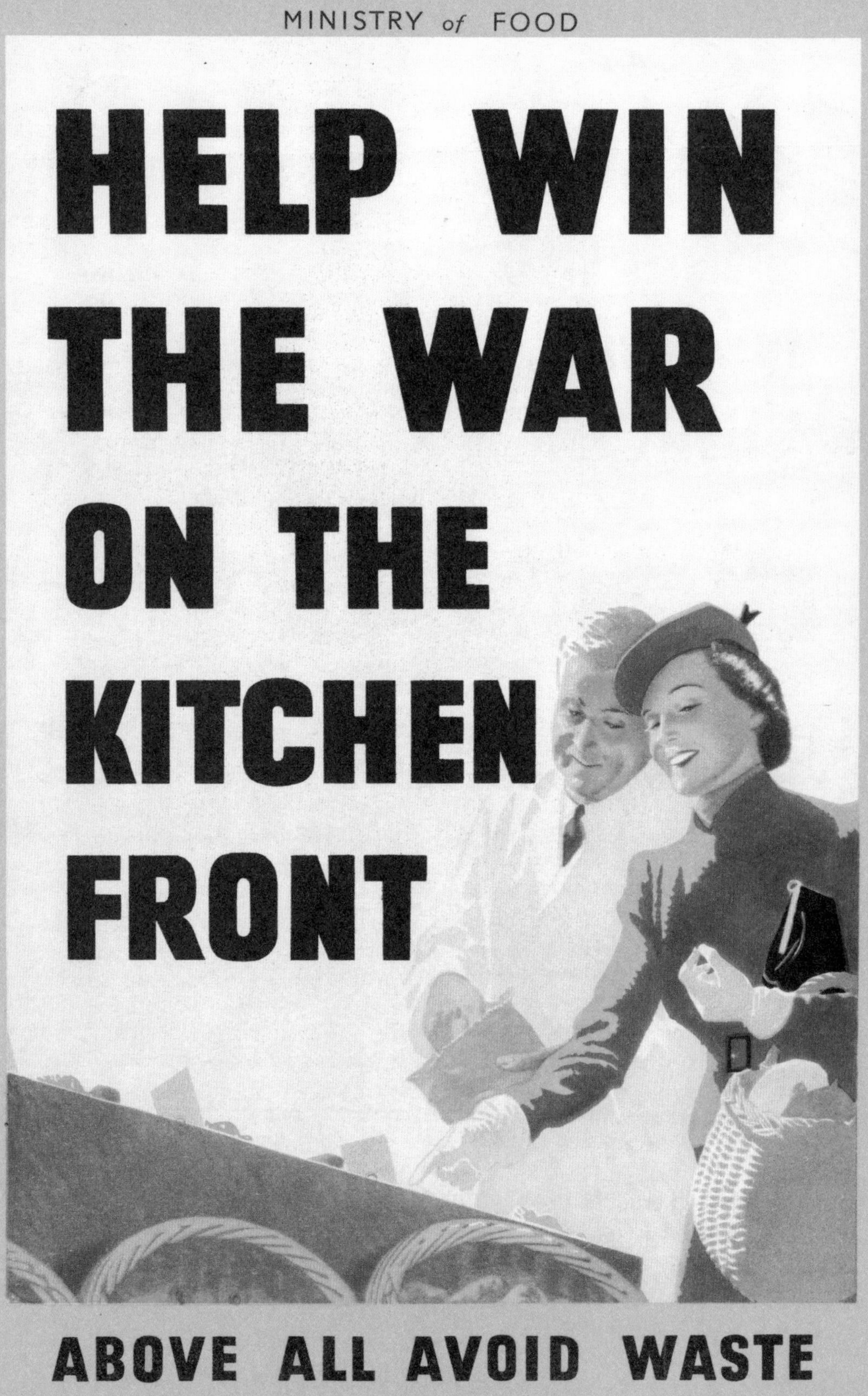
MINISTRY of FOOD
HELP WIN THE WAR ON THE KITCHEN FRONT
ABOVE ALL AVOID WASTE

MINISTRY *of* FOOD

Let your SHOPPING help our SHIPPING

PLAN YOUR MEALS TO AVOID WASTE

problem, and almost everyone suffered from chilblains.

Entertainment came via the wireless. As well as anxiously tuning in for the latest news, women at home enjoyed listening to such programmes as *Workers' Playtime*, a lunchtime programme of music and entertainment broadcast from a different workplace each time; and *ITMA (It's That Man Again)*, starring Britain's favourite radio comedian, Tommy Handley. Or you might take your torch (if you could get batteries – they were in short supply) to guide you through the blackout to the local pub or cinema. There was a cinema on every high street and most managed to remain open throughout the war. 'Going to the pictures' was a welcome escape from the worries of daily life.

In cities fear of air raids was ever present. When a siren sounded the air raid warning, people would dash out of the house to their back garden, to take refuge in the Anderson shelter if they had one. This was a corrugated steel shelter partially dug down into the ground and covered over with a thick layer of earth. Others would make their way to public shelters, for example in the London tube train stations. One family used their downstairs bathroom as a shelter because it had only one small window and outside walls 47cm (18½in) thick. Washing things, first aid kit and other items recommended in an Air Raid Precautions (ARP) booklet were kept permanently in the bathroom and when there was a raid, the family would take in a tin of Smiths potato crisps, three bottles of lemonade, several bars of chocolate and some old magazines to read. There they would stay until the all clear sounded.

FAR FROM HOME

The evacuation of women and children to the countryside changed the lives of both evacuees and their hosts, sometimes for the better. A farmer's wife who took in two children said what a pleasure it was to see them enjoying the fresh air and having a life away from the bombs and shortages.

One boy evacuated from South London to a farm in Devon had never, at the age of 11, seen a cow. As far as he knew, milk appeared in bottles on the doorstep, and he was completely thrilled to see a cow being milked. He loved to observe the changing seasons and the tasks that went with them from ploughing with horses, to haymaking and harvest time when first the corn and then the orchard fruits were gathered in. One of his jobs was to keep the heifers away from the apples in the orchard. After returning to the city he looked back with pleasure on a life lived close to the land, dedicated to the production of food.

Country life didn't suit all townies. Some of the women evacuated with their children complained about having to walk two or three miles to the shops. When they got there they found prices were higher than at the Co-ops and chain grocers they were used to. They couldn't buy ready-cooked food and those who had gas at home hated cooking on the coal ranges in the country. They grumbled because buses to the nearest town only ran every two hours, and the bus stop might be as much as

3 miles away. How could a girl get her hair permed? Where could she go to the cinema? 'I'd rather be bombed on my own doorstep than stay here and die of depression,' said one.

Some of the village people, for their part, thought the evacuees dirty and their clothes unsuitable and flashy. The women were heard to swear like men and, (shock, horror!), some were seen going into the pub. When children came by themselves, they soon adapted to their new surroundings and became part of the family, but when their mothers accompanied them, the mums found fault with everything, and the children took their cue from them and were difficult to manage. 'I'd never have a woman I've never seen dumped on me – I'd rather have three children,' said one village host.

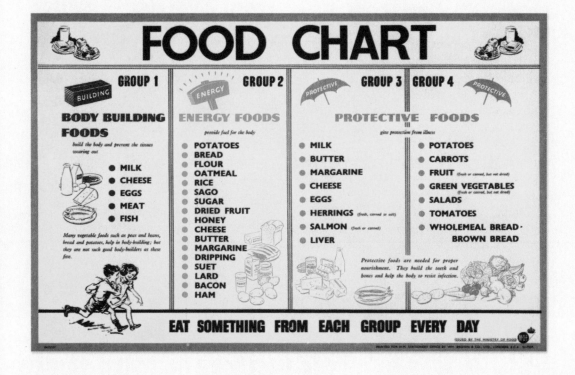

MILK THE BACKBONE OF YOUNG BRITAIN

Nevertheless, many lasting friendships were formed. One evacuee remembers that, after returning to London in 1946, when food was even scarcer than before, every Christmas for several years the farmer on whom they had been billeted would send 'a big brown parcel containing a leg of pork and as much food as he could cram round it, which we were sure he wasn't supposed to do.' Others stayed in touch for the rest of their lives.

Others living far from home included men and women serving in the forces, Land Girls and prisoners of war. Land Girls didn't have to buy or cook their own food, but were catered for by the farmer's wife, their landlady, or in hostels. Most had no complaints. One girl recorded with satisfaction having a poached egg for tea, ham for supper, and bread, butter and jam, cake and biscuits, all home-made, at both meals.

An 18-year-old German PoW, interviewed a lifetime later, remembered how he would be taken by truck from the prison camp in Devon to the farm where he worked. He was made welcome and treated as one of the family. At the end of the working day the truck took him back for a hot meal, usually a stew of potatoes with some meat, peas, beans and carrots and two slices of bread, and occasionally a generous helping of fish and chips instead.

THE STUFF TO GIVE THE TROOPS

Whilst the civilian population's rations were designed to be enough (just!) to keep people healthy, those in the armed services, and in vital occupations such as mining, were given extra rations. Lieut-Commander Mason, wrote home from sea in September 1941:

'You asked me what [the food] was like and if it was better than college [Royal Naval College Dartmouth]. Well it is. We have meat every day and always a choice... Unfortunately we can't keep cows on board so we have no fresh milk. The other day I went ashore and drank fresh creamy milk for about an hour!'

But Edward Stebbing, a soldier stationed at Sheffield, was not so lucky. He complained that hot meals were not always available, and supplies were disrupted by air raids. As a result, he spent much of his money on food. 'Woolworth's is the best place to go. Went there today and had two sausages, an egg and chips, bread and butter, tea and a sweet for only 1/11 – the best meal I have had since I've been here. The cooking is done by electricity.'

Service men and women and civilian war workers sometimes ate at canteens, some of which were better than others. A volunteer working in a YMCA canteen wrote, 'When the war is over no one is going to look at a sausage again'. High tea at the YMCA was invariably sausage and mash, and 'If a soldier says he simply cannot eat sausages, they say, "we will prepare a rissole specially for you."' Out of sight, the cook would then skin a sausage, reshape the inside and fry it.

American troops somehow managed to make sure that toasted spam sandwiches were on canteen menus, and Joan Charles, a civil servant working for the Ministry of Agriculture in Lancashire, who wrote regularly to her fiance

Tony Ross in the RAF in North Africa, described how she cooked as a volunteer at a new Red Cross canteen at Lytham. It catered mainly for Americans and became known as 'The Doughnut Dive'. 'I spent three hours deep in washing

BETTER POT-LUCK
with Churchill today

THAN HUMBLE PIE
under Hitler tomorrow

DON'T WASTE FOOD!

up and frying doughnuts... the kitchen gets so hot it reminds me of pictures I have seen of stoke holds in ships! I wonder rather wistfully if Americans eat doughnuts in summer, but fear their capacity is unaffected by anything! It is a source of unending wonder to me that anyone can eat six of these stodgy, fatty, uninteresting lumps!'

A few years later, when I was old enough to walk to school, one of my treats was to stop on the way home and spend my pocket money on a doughnut. I still have a weakness for them.

Perhaps the most important service provided by mobile canteens was to feed people who had lost their homes in bombing raids. The morale of the civilian population was critical to the war effort and hot food was found to be of great importance in keeping up the morale of victims of the blitz.

Comforting hot food and, above all, endless cups of tea were provided by the Women's Voluntary Service (WVS) at temporary feeding stations and mobile canteens. My grandmother was a volunteer and I remember her bustling about with military briskness, wearing her WVS uniform. It consisted of a green Harris tweed suit, with a matching 'porkpie' hat, rather grandly designed by Norman Hartnell, the Queen's couturier.

Volunteering for such war work put an additional burden on women but they were proud to play their part, and many drove themselves till they came close to total exhaustion.

NOT HOARDING

For those living in the country, Britain was still a land of plenty, and it is true that in many farming communities fresh produce was always available and the rigours of rationing were hardly felt.

In the cities it was a different story. In 1939 it was already certain that food rationing would come in the event of war, and people considered it prudent to stock up on tins and other foods with a long shelf life. Those who felt uneasy about hoarding were reassured as early as 2 February 1939, when the President of the Board of Trade announced in Parliament, 'I see no objection to the accumulation by householders in peace time of small reserves of suitable food-stuffs equivalent to about one week's normal requirements. Household reserves of this kind would constitute a useful addition to the total stocks of the country.'

So, far from being regarded as hoarding, filling the cupboard under the stairs with tins of food became a sensible precaution.

From now on queuing became a normal part of shopping. In August one woman, after queuing for half an hour, came home triumphant with six tins of new potatoes, three of baked beans, ½lb coffee and ½lb sugar. In the grocers' shops displays of tinned goods rose overnight like mountain ranges after a volcanic eruption, but quickly disappeared again as householders stocked up. When the blackout began torches and batteries were also snapped up as soon as they appeared.

UNCLE FRED

'A cheerful cove'
Geoffrey Dawson
'A dear man'
Lord Rea

The spirits of voluntary workers and the population in general were kept up by a strong publicity campaign instigated by the Minister of Food, Lord Woolton.

Born Frederick James Marquis, he was educated at Manchester Grammar School and Manchester University. He became a social worker and, later on, a very successful businessman, running a chain of department stores and being made a peer in 1939 for his contribution to British industry. He took the title Baron Woolton and served on various government committees.

In April 1940 Woolton was appointed Minister of Food by Prime Minister Neville Chamberlain. The following month Winston Churchill became Prime Minister and kept Woolton in his post.

Woolton's remarkable personal qualities made him ideal for the job. Imposing restrictions and overseeing rationing are unlikely to endear one to the public, yet he was universally trusted and regarded with affection. He became known to the public as Uncle Fred. People became so fond of Uncle Fred that they would, for example, write to thank him for arranging extra milk for babies and nursing mothers: 'A few of their wives sent me photographs of their babies, apparently bursting with food and good health,' he wrote in his memoirs, 'But it was thoughtless of so many to write on the photograph "One of Lord Woolton's babies!"'

He used his exceptional organisational skills to implement and promote the complex food rationing system and ensure that its nationwide application ran smoothly.

He also had a remarkable gift for propaganda and public relations, 'I found the Ministry of Food suffering from a general depression', he wrote in his memoirs. 'The press was against them and they were dejected, and frankly puzzled, by their unpopularity.' His first step was to restore morale by visiting his staff in their offices and by inviting the King to tour his Ministry, which raised its public standing.

As well as Dig for Victory he masterminded a massive advertising campaign, urging the public to fight the war on The Kitchen Front. This was the name of a five-minute radio programme, which followed the 8am news. Woolton asked the popular comic duo, Gert and Daisy to broadcast on the programme and make people laugh about food rationing. They did.

He himself would broadcast when there were changes to the rations (usually for the worse) to be announced. He attached great importance to these occasions. 'I always kept a picture in front of my mind of the man in a cottage house, sitting without a collar, with slippers on, at the end of the day's work, with children playing on the rug, with his wife washing-up in an adjoining room with the door open. To prepare this simple broadcast, lasting for twelve and a half minutes, I rarely spent less than eight hours.'

Leaflets offering recipes for cooking the limited range of food available under rationing were part of the campaign to keep the nation healthy and morale high. One such recipe first appeared on the menu at the Savoy Hotel in London, entitled 'Le Lord Woolton Pie'. Those who cooked it at home and ate it were not impressed, but their affection for him was undiminished.

A victim commented: 'I just can't believe that such a wonderful man could have given his name to such a dish.'

When Woolton died on 14 December 1964, Lord Longford, paying tribute to him in the House of Lords, described him as 'a many-sided man of far reaching talents and achievements, but... basically all of one piece and simple. His was a singularly outgoing nature, dedicated to service public and private, wherever the call might come. It came to him naturally to like, indeed to love, his fellow human beings. It was his reward... that he was liked by all and loved by a great many.

On the same occasion, Lord Carrington said that 'Uncle Fred' was indeed like 'a favourite uncle who was generous and kind, shrewd and wise and full of good advice... fun to be with, fascinating to listen to.'

The food rationing system and the changes in agriculture were aimed at ensuring a healthy diet for all – and it was something of a triumph for the government in general and Lord Woolton in particular that, by the end of the war, they had come close to achieving it. The health of the population, and particularly that of the children, was better at the end of the war than it had been at the start. Everyone got their share, and the changes in agriculture meant that people ate much less meat, fat and sugar, and many more vegetables.

Déjeuner 8/6

Les Hors d'Œuvre Variés

ou

POTAGES

Consommé Julienne   St. Germain

‡ Crustacés ~~ŒUFS~~, et FARINEUX.

Œuf ~~plat~~ Bercy   Gnocchis de Semoule au Gratin   Omelette Fines Herbes

LES PLATS DU JOUR

* Le Turbotin Coquelin
Turbot with White Wine Sauce, garnished with sliced Potatoes. Glaced.

* Le Hareng grillé.   Sce. Moutarde
Grilled Soft Roe Herring.   Mustard Sauce.

* La Raie au Beurre Noir
Skate fried in Butter with Capers

* La Côte de Bœuf rôtie, Yorkshire
Roast Rib of Beef. Yorkshire Pudding. Horseradish Sauce.

* Le Coq au Vin de Bourgogne
Spring Chicken cooked with Red Wine and Mushrooms.

* Les Tripes grillées, Sauce Tartare
Tripes grilled. Tartar Sauce.

Le Lord Woolton Pie
Pie of sliced Potatoes and Carrots seasoned with Herbs.

LEGUMES.

Petits Pois Bleus   Haricots Verts   Choux de Bruxelles
Choux à l'Anglaise   Pommes Nouvelles   Pommes Sautées

ENTREMETS.

Le Pouding Tapioca   Le Treflé Ecossaise
La Bande Normande   Les Pommes Meringuées

‡ By agreement with the Ministry of Food, only one dish of Meat, Fish or Poultry may be served at a meal.

SAVOY RESTAURANT   JEUDI. 6 MARS 1941

Making the most
of the meat

CHAPTER 4

Getting Your Rations

Conversation between two grown-up sisters before
going to sleep:
Jenny : I did the most awful thing today... I hardly
dare tell you... The most awful, terrible thing, simply
atrocious, I can't think why I did it, my dear.
Muriel: Go on, tell me the worst, quick.
Jenny: It's been on my mind all day... It's really terrible
but what do you think I did? When I made that cake
I made a mistake and made it with the butter ration
instead of the margarine.
Muriel: You fool!... three whole ounces!
Muriel Green, 4 December 1940

Food rationing came as no surprise. Since early in 1939 people had been anticipating war and expecting rationing as part of it. Britain declared war on Germany on 3 September, and on the 8th the Ministry of Food was established, becoming the sole buyer and importer of food. It was also responsible, as the entire nation soon found out, for the introduction and supervision of food rationing.

During the First World War, food prices went up by 60 per cent, so that shortages affected the poor more than the rich. Since then it had been clear that in the event of another war, rationing would have to be introduced. During the Munich Crisis in 1938, when war seemed inevitable, the British Government started to make its plans. Its aim was to organise rationing in such a way that it would not only prevent starvation, but would ensure a healthy workforce. If the system was fair, people would unite in making the best of a difficult time, and morale would remain high.

The need for rationing soon became evident. Almost immediately after war was declared, Germany's U-boats started to attack British merchant ships. Six months later losses were averaging 400,000 tons a month, with devastating effects on food cargoes.

HOW RATIONING WORKED

In September 1939 a National Register was set up and everybody was issued with an identity card. On 29 November, the first Minister of Food, William Morrison, announced that rationing would start on 8 January 1940.

Each person was issued with a ration book in one of six categories:

GENERAL:
for adults and children over six

CHILD'S BOOK:
for under sixes

TRAVELLER'S:
for salesmen, lorry drivers, actors

EMERGENCY BOOK:
for those bombed out of their homes

SERVICE PERSONNEL BOOK:
for use while on leave

SEAMAN'S WEEKLY BOOK

Vegetarians and those who didn't eat dairy foods or eggs had to register with their local Food Office and vegetarians were then issued with a special ration book entitling them to extra eggs, cheese and nuts, instead of meat. Vegans were similarly allowed appropriate extra rations.

'Margaret's dog Dandy has been accustomed to a bar of Cadbury's milk chocolate a day and declines to accept any other make or flavour. Dandy has always had his dog biscuits spread thickly with butter and now has Margaret's rations. He takes six fresh eggs a week and has his helpings of liver daily. Catering for Dandy's needs is becoming an issue.' (Pam Ashford 19th September 1940).

The general book was buff in colour, the children's blue. If you lost your book it was extremely difficult to get it replaced, the process involving a great deal of queuing at bureaucrats' desks. Diarist Kathleen Tipper wrote, 'Our ration books have turned up, having been lost at the branch on Friday. We had to go to all the trouble of applying at the food office for new books, get our

Typical Adult Weekly Rations

BACON & HAM	4oz
BUTTER	2oz
CHEESE	2oz
MARGARINE	4oz
COOKING FAT	4oz, often dropping to 2oz
MILK	3pt, but not always
SUGAR	8oz
PRESERVES	1lb every two months
TEA	2oz
EGGS	one shell egg a week if available
DRIED EGGS	one pack per month (equivalent to 12 eggs)
SWEETS	12oz a month

Plus a monthly points scheme for fish, meat, fruit or peas

forms signed at the police station, and then the wretched branch manager rang Joyce [her sister] today to say that they had turned up. I am glad but what a lot of trouble their carelessness has given.'

My own mother kept the family's ration books in the drawer of the kitchen table, taking them out every time she shopped and replacing them on her return. Vague and scatty in other respects, she never departed from this routine.

Once you had your ration book, you had to register with a supplier for each of the rationed items. Once registered, you had to stick with your chosen grocer, milkman or butcher, so it was an important choice. If you had a good relationship with your butcher

he might save a few sausages for you, or, if there were no other customers about, disappear into the back of the shop to bring you out a couple of lambs' kidneys wrapped in their suet. Sausages and offal, such as kidneys, liver, brains and tripe were 'off the ration' and in theory made a nourishing alternative to the popular cuts of beef, lamb or pork, but in practice they were often in short supply and only available if you queued for them. The meat ration was reckoned not by weight, as with other produce, but by price.

In March 1940 the meat ration was 1s 10d worth, per person per week (half that for children under six). This would buy almost 3lb of beef, pork or mutton, or 2lb of stewing steak, or five pork chops. No hardship in these quantities, even for a nation of dedicated carnivores, but by June 1941 the ration had been almost halved. Rationing by price meant that you got better value if you bought skirt of beef or lamb's breast rather than steak or chops.

Date Items Came Off the Ration List

BREAD	July 1948
JAM	December 1948
POINTS SYSTEM ENDED	May 1950
TEA	October 1952
SWEETS	February 1953
EGGS	March 1953
SUGAR	September 1953
BUTTER, CHEESE, MARGARINE & COOKING FATS	May 1954
MEAT & BACON	June 1954

LANCASHIRE HOTPOT

Serves 4

It still pays to find a good local butcher and to get to know him (or her). Take their advice about the best cheap cuts and how to cook them. Middle neck lamb chops and kidneys can save you money and add huge flavour to this hearty hotpot.

25g (1oz) butter, dripping or oil, for frying
1 onion, sliced
1 bay leaf
750g (1lb 10oz) potatoes, peeled and thinly sliced
600g (1lb 5oz) middle neck lamb chops
4–5 tablespoons plain flour

2 lamb's kidneys, quartered and the core removed
2 carrots, peeled and chopped
1 turnip, peeled and diced
1½ teaspoons Worcestershire sauce
500ml (17fl oz) stock or water
salt and freshly ground black pepper

Preheat the oven to 200°C (400°F) gas mark 6.

Heat the fat in a frying pan and gently fry the onion until soft.

Put the onion, bay leaf and half the potatoes in a large, deep casserole.

Season the flour with salt and pepper. Dust the chops in the flour. Brown the chops in the frying pan, in batches. Arrange them over the potatoes in the casserole.

Flour and brown the kidneys and tuck them in around the chops. Add the carrots and turnip, filling in any gaps. Add the Worcestershire sauce to the stock or water, and bring to the boil.

Meanwhile, arrange the rest of the potatoes in overlapping circles on top of the meat and vegetables. Pour the hot stock over the potatoes until they are just covered.

Cover with a lid and put in the preheated oven. After 20 minutes, turn the oven down to 150°C (275°F) gas mark 1 and cook for 1½ hours. Remove the lid for the last 30 minutes to let the potatoes brown.

Rationing meant extra work for shopkeepers. In Colyton at War, a fascinating book about wartime in a small East Devon town, Gordon White recalls helping his father in his grocery shop. '[My father] was a stickler for getting everything just right... You couldn't be a fraction out. Father made sure we understood that the tiniest discrepancy one way was unfair to the customer, and unlawful, and the other way costly to us. People were entitled to precise weights and that's what they paid for. We closed for the week at Sunday lunchtime. People's ration coupons were spread out on the dining table... threaded in 50s or 100s on to little pieces of cardboard in their separate colours, buff for this, pink for that, green for the other. Once a month they were taken to the Ministry of Food offices in Axminster and exchanged for the next month's allocation of commodities. Whatever you had sold one month would be allowed to you the next.'

Lord Woolton, the new Minister of Food, was quick to get his propaganda machine working, issuing Food Facts (published in the newspapers), and cookery leaflets. His first message was a personal one, appealing for help in defeating 'the enemy's attempt to starve us out'. He promised, through rationing and price control, to see that everyone got a fair share of essential foods at fair prices, adding, 'Now, here is your part in the fight for victory. When a particular food is not available, cheerfully accept something else – home produced if possible. Keep loyally to the rationing regulations.

'Above all – whether you are shopping, cooking or eating – remember "Food is a Munition of War". Don't waste it.'

He urged people to eat plenty of potatoes and oatmeal but leave cheese (as yet un-rationed) for vegetarians, miners and others who did heavy manual work.

HERRINGS IN OATMEAL

Serves 4

The basic ration required to sustain a healthy population was worked out with advice from Sir Jack Drummond, a distinguished nutritionist. One of his recommendations was that the nation should be fed on wholemeal bread, herrings, raw vegetables and dried eggs. He explained that a man with a pint of beer in one hand and a plate of herrings and fried potatoes in the other was getting 2,400 calories, which was adequate nourishment.

8 tablespoons fine or medium oatmeal
salt and freshly ground black pepper
4 double herring fillets

2–3 tablespoons dripping or cooking oil
lemon wedges, to serve
chopped parsley, to serve

Spread the oatmeal on a plate and season it with salt and pepper. Coat each herring fillet with the seasoned oatmeal, pressing the oatmeal onto the fish with your hands.

Heat a thin film of dripping or oil in a large frying pan. Put the herrings in with the skin side uppermost. Fry for 6–8 minutes, until lightly browned, turning once. Depending on the size of your pan, you may need to fry the fish in batches.

Drain on kitchen paper and serve with lemon wedges and chopped parsley if liked.

Drummond's advice was not followed, nor was a proposal for a 'basal diet' consisting of 1lb potatoes, 12oz bread, 6oz vegetables, 2oz oatmeal, 1oz fat and just over 1.2 pints milk. Winston Churchill took an interest in rationing proposals and rejected the basal diet, writing to Lord Woolton, 'The way to lose the war is to try to force the British public into a diet of milk, oatmeal, potatoes, etc, washed down on gala occasions with a little lime juice.' When told that people were complaining about the small meat ration, Churchill asked to see it. When shown a week's ration, he said it would be quite enough for him. He thought the ration was for a single meal.

Drummond was a distinguished scientist and his work was important. He lobbied successfully for the National Loaf and for free fruit juice for children. One of my earliest memories was being given a compulsory spoonful of cod liver oil (free but disgusting), followed by rose hip syrup (also compulsory but absolutely delicious).

Drummond also reorganised school meals, basing them on an adequate supply of vitamins, and devised a liquid mixture of protein, glucose and vitamins for intravenous injection, which saved the lives of many concentration camp victims at the end of the war. His own diet, he said, consisted of 'what my wife gives me and it's always very good'.

THE POINTS SYSTEM

Various foods could be bought with points, which were outside the fixed categories of weekly rations such as meat, cheese or fat. The points system was devised partly to control the supply of various foods, partly to boost morale by offering a degree of choice, and partly to correct a perceived unfairness. Although most people considered rationing fair, there was some grumbling that the high prices of 'off the ration' items, such as tinned fruit, dried fruit, breakfast cereals and biscuits favoured the rich shopper over the poor.

Each ration book holder was allocated a number of points that could be used each month to buy items the Ministry designated as 'on points'. The system gave the Ministry flexibility to change the list of foods available on points each month and the amount allocated.

There was usually a scramble to use up your points before the period expired. 'The points period ends on Saturday and we have three books to complete,' wrote diarist Pam Ashford in July 1942. 'I gave mother two and said to her to see what she could do at Miss Maclean's and they gave her a tin of American meat, a large tin of salmon, a small tin of sardines and tin of Beefex. That used 24 [points]. I think it was a good choice. I took the third book into town and got half a pound of dates and 1lb prunes. I think I shall use the remaining eight on Weetabix.'

Nella Last, who described herself as a talented shopper, had nothing but scorn for those less gifted. She wrote, 'I saw women with several tins – large ones – in their baskets, which must have taken about all the month's points for the family! I met... a policeman's wife. She was very jubilant over two small and one large tins of salmon. She said, "I've not had first-grade salmon for months and I grabbed the chance." Idly I said, "how many points are they?" and got the amazing answer, "Thirty-two the large and twenty each the small ones" – she had spent all but eight points on them!'

OFF THE RATION

Those who had a garden or allotment and kept hens or even a pig, found it easier to make their rations last out the week than others. As shipping losses continued, it became more and more important to find ways to supplement the basic ration.

The meat ration started at 1s 10d but in March 1941 it was reduced to 1s, returning to 1s 2d in July, the price it remained at for the rest of the war.

TOAD IN THE HOLE

Serves 4

Even wartime sausages with their low meat content could not spoil this dish, a favourite at school dinners as well as at home. It will be even better if you buy the best sausages you can get and make sure the fat is really hot before the batter goes in. Serve the dish as soon as it is cooked, before it deflates.

125g (4½oz) flour
3 medium eggs and 1 extra
   egg white
300ml (10½fl oz) whole milk

2 tablespoons oil
salt and freshly ground black
   pepper
8 best pork sausages

Preheat the oven to 220°C (425°F) gas mark 7.

Put the flour, eggs, milk and seasoning in a blender and pulse in 10-second bursts until the batter is smooth. Leave the plunger off to help aeration. Let the batter rest for half an hour.

Put the oil in a baking tin and heat it in the oven for 5 minutes. Add the sausages and cook for a few minutes, until the fat runs and they are lightly browned.

Pour the batter around the sausages in the tin and bake in the preheated oven for about 20 minutes until the batter is risen and golden brown. Check after 15 minutes.

Tomato ketchup is almost obligatory with Toad in the Hole.

Variations: Make individual toads in muffin tins, using chipolatas cut in three.

As a result unrationed meat prices increased, calves liver going up from 2/- to 2/8d a pound. It was at this time that the Ministry promoted recipes for Woolton Pie and other meat-free dishes.

Sheep's heart remained something of a bargain at 9d (up from 6d). Nella Last, who we already know as a good manager and a keen cook, let her soldier son, home for the weekend, choose the menu: sausages 'fried brown and crisp and not soggy with fat' for dinner. For tea she proposed a chop or fillet of plaice but he asked for braised lambs' hearts with tiny onions and lots of hot toast – 'the cheapest thing possible. It was always their Saturday tea in winter when schoolboys.'

There are other excellent kinds of offal for today's adventurous cooks. I remember eating brains at an early age and not enjoying them. Even when urged by my granny to 'think of all the poor children starving in Russia' I found each mouthful hard to swallow. But I recently tried pig's brains on toast and found them delicious.

In the summer of 1940 Lord Woolton announced that tea would be rationed to 2oz per person per week. This was reckoned to make between 20 and 25 cups of tea – difficult for an addict to make last a whole week, and those who liked their tea good and sweet also found it hard to eke out their weekly 8oz of sugar. Those who tried sweetening their tea with honey or golden syrup, found it turned the tea very black and gave it a strange taste. Instead they bought saccharine or Sugarettes, a sugar substitute available at health food shops.

The rationing of sweets and chocolate caused much anguish. In our house the sweetie tin came out after lunch and we were allowed one square of chocolate each, or one boiled sweet. My husband had a friend at school who, by shaving his Mars Bar with a razor blade into wafer thin slices, could make it last a week or longer.

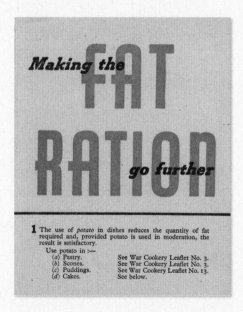

Making the **FAT RATION** *go further*

1 The use of *potato* in dishes reduces the quantity of fat required and, provided potato is used in moderation, the result is satisfactory.

Use potato in :—
(a) Pastry.	See War Cookery Leaflet No. 3.
(b) Scones.	See War Cookery Leaflet No. 3.
(c) Puddings.	See War Cookery Leaflet No. 13.
(d) Cakes.	See below.

CHOCOLATE TRUFFLES

Makes 45 truffles

A friend remembers making chocolate truffles from a mixture of cocoa powder, margarine and mashed potato. Fortunately this peacetime recipe avoids such extreme austerity.

270ml (9½fl oz) double cream
350g (12oz) dark chocolate,
  broken into small chunks

25g (1oz) butter
1–2 tablespoons cocoa powder

In a heavy-based saucepan heat the cream over a gentle heat. Do not let it boil. Remove from the heat and add the chocolate. Stir until melted. Stir in the butter, then leave the mixture to cool and firm up.

Shape into balls. Roll the truffles in the cocoa powder, coating thoroughly.

The truffles can be kept in an airtight container in the fridge for up to 3 days.

PEPPERMINT CREAMS

Makes lots of sweets (about 450g/1lb)

This is a great recipe to make with children as it involves absolutely no cooking.

1 egg white
1 teaspoon lemon juice
400–425g (14–15oz) icing sugar,
   plus extra to dust

a few drops of peppermint extract
small pastry cutters

In a large bowl, lightly beat the egg white. Add the lemon juice and gradually mix in the icing sugar to make a smooth, firm dough. Add the peppermint extract, a drop at a time, until it tastes right.

Dust a work surface with icing sugar. Using a rolling pin also dusted with icing sugar, roll out the mixture to about 1cm (½ inch) thick.

Use small pastry cutters to cut out into rounds or other shapes and leave to dry on a large baking tray lined with baking paper.

For some, the rigours of rationing were alleviated by informal barter, which could come perilously close to black marketeering (see Chapter 5), but was mostly harmless enough. One diarist notes in September 1943, 'saw Mrs Greenslade, and a nice fat cockerel was transferred from her car to ours, plus a glorious bowl of dead-black blackberries, while a basket of pears and a few apples went from our car to hers... it's just fine to be giving something away that one has grown in one's own garden'. A few weeks later another wrote, 'killed senior hen. Bartered her for 6lb onions.'

Those with relations abroad had the occasional excitement of a food parcel to supplement their rations. One family regularly received goodies from a relation in Florida, including honey, kumquats in syrup, guava jelly and chocolate. Customs duty was levied on parcels from abroad, but the recipients thought half a crown duty 'not excessive' for a parcel of dried fruit, tinned olives, chocolate and Dutch cheese.

It was useful to have someone serving in the Royal Navy. Kathleen Tippett wrote in her diary that her brother Philip returned from a tour of duty with 'tins of fat, several tins of jam, some tinned fruit, tinned meat, a Christmas pudding, some tomato juice, condensed milk, soup, starch, boiled sweets, Turkish delight, six tennis balls, two hot water bottles, and eight ounces of wool each for Joyce and I. Also a tinned picnic ham weighing 9lb 7oz – we will have a party to use that. He also brought six jellies, mixed fruit, honey and lemon butter – and the sight of it all on the dining room table made one's eyes almost pop out.'

Lemons were unobtainable in Britain, and men in the forces serving in Italy or Sicily would sometimes send a few home. 'Used one for hot lemonade with rum at bedtime,' a recipient recorded.

Sometimes the American forces, always better fed than their British allies, would donate provisions to be raffled at a social evening. One such parcel contained, among other things, a bar of chocolate, a tin of Ovaltine, cough sweets, tea, a packet of grated cheese and soup powder. A total of 9s 6d was raised.

EATING OUT

To lessen the hardship of rationing, the government encouraged people to eat out at least once a month and to have their main meals at school or at work. Before the war school dinners had been available to just 250,000 children, but by the end almost all children had dinner at school, nearly 1,850,000 a day. There was a similar increase in factory canteens; firms over a certain size were legally obliged to provide them and the number went from 1,500 in 1939 to 18,500 in 1945.

To make cheap, nutritious meals available to city workers, the Ministry arranged for local authorities to set up 'British Restaurants' to provide cheap, nourishing meals. These were served in premises such as church halls and working men's clubs. You paid in advance and were given little coloured discs of different colours for your main course and pudding. Some schools (mine was one) had their dinners sent round from the local British Restaurant in huge metal trays. Sometimes the system broke down and we would all put on our coats, hats and gloves and troop round to the British Restaurant in a crocodile. The meat was grey, gristly and fatty. It was hard to know whether we were eating beef or mutton. It was served with mashed potato (grey and lumpy) and cabbage (fibrous and watery).

Perhaps we were just unlucky. Out of 2,000 British Restaurants serving more than half a million meals a day, some earned praise. One first-timer went for lunch and was surprised and delighted to be asked, 'Are you hungry sir?' On replying that he was, he was given an exceptionally generous helping. The service was quick and the helpers very courteous. Another diarist gave Lord Woolton the credit for a 'V.G lunch at British restaurant: stuffed lamb, potatoes, cabbage; date roll and custard, cup of tea, all for 11d. I have thought for a long while, that Lord Woolton is one of the ablest Ministers in the present Government.'

Hotels and restaurants were not obliged to observe rationing rules, or to collect coupons from their customers' ration books. Not everyone agreed with this policy. Nella Last, on an outing to Morecambe in March 1942 was shocked and surprised at the lavish restaurant meals served: cooked teas with sausages, fish or chops with chips. She thought the people tucking in should be made to give up ration coupons. 'Coupons had to be given up in the last war for meat meals – why not in this?'

At top London restaurants the rich could eat extremely well. Their conspicuous consumption generated such resentment among those who could not afford the prices that, from 1942, the government prohibited restaurants from charging more than 5s a meal. Some establishments got round this by charging an extra 7s 6d cover charge or charging extra for flowers on the table, or for a live band.

Overleaf is a representation of the Dorchester dinner menu of 29 November 1940 which marked 603 Squadron's claim of 100 enemy aircraft destroyed during the Battle of Britain.

Menu

Huîtres native
Saumon d'ecosse fumé

Coupe de tortue verte
Brindilles diablées
Crème ambassadeur

Flan aux fruits de mer à la mode de paimpo

Faisan rôti à l'anglaise
Coeur de celeri au jus
Pommes fondants

Poire roxane
Biscuits secs

Café

POTAGE CRÈME AMBASSADEUR

Serves 8–10

The Dorchester's grandly named Crème Ambassadeur is a variation on a homely, filling split pea soup my mother used to make, with bacon, sorrel (hard to obtain but easy to grow in the garden) and lettuce. Instead of chopped bacon (on the ration) she added bacon rinds for flavour and removed them after cooking, and instead of cream she had to use 'top of milk'.

400g (14oz) dried split peas
60g (2¹/₄oz) butter
1 carrot, diced
1 onion, finely sliced
85g (3oz) bacon, chopped
2 leeks (white part only),
 finely sliced
1 garlic clove, peeled and crushed
1 litre (1³/₄ pts) chicken stock

1 bouquet garni
salt and freshly ground pepper
80ml (2½fl oz) double cream
85g (3oz) lettuce, shredded
85g (3oz) sorrel or spinach,
 thinly shredded
chopped chervil or parsley,
 to garnish

Soak the split peas overnight in cold water, then drain and set aside.

Melt half the butter in a large saucepan over a low heat. Add the carrot, onion, bacon, leeks and garlic and cook, stirring occasionally, until they are soft but not coloured.

Add the drained peas and the chicken stock. Bring to the boil, add the bouquet garni and simmer gently for 40 minutes.

Purée the soup in a blender. Then tip it back into the saucepan and add the cream. Season to taste.

Heat the remaining butter in a saucepan over a low heat. Add the lettuce and sorrel or spinach and cook gently for a few minutes until wilted.

Add the wilted leaves to the hot soup. Serve garnished with chervil or parsley.

Yorkshireman Kenneth Thornton Roberts was called up for military service on 15 February 1940 and served in 246 Field Company, Royal Engineers, initially as a carpenter and joiner. His daughter told me he became a cook after suffering a back injury. Towards the end of the war he served in Palestine. His handwritten army recipe book includes stalwart nourishing dishes such as Chop or Sausage Toad in the Hole, Curryed (sic) Beef, and three robust vegetable soups. The quantities given in his recipes are all for 100 men. His book also includes plans for making home-made ovens and a chart showing the daily and weekly ration for each man.

HOUSEHOLD SOUP

serves 10

This recipe is adapted from one in Kath Leadbeater's recipe book 'When its brown it's done…' It come's from the army notebook of her father, Yorkshireman Kenneth Thornton Roberts. I have reduced his recipe for 100 men to quantities suitable for 10. Half can be frozen for future use. It is just the kind of warming soup my mother used to make, using whatever vegetables were in season. The key to success is a good, strong home-made stock. To get meaty stock bones in rationing days you would need to be on good terms with your butcher, and that relationship is still important today.

2 oz fat or oil
6 ½ oz onions peeled and chopped
6 ½ oz carrots, diced
2 leeks, washed and sliced across
1 lb potatoes, peeled and diced
4 oz celery, sliced

8 oz lentils
1 seasoning faggot (bouquet garni)
5 pints stock made with beef bones,
   vegetables and herbs
Salt and pepper

In a large saucepan melt the fat or oil and sweat the vegetables in it over a gentle heat for 5 minutes. Add the lentils and stock and bring to the boil. Simmer gently until the vegetables are tender (about 30 minutes). Season to taste and serve hot.

Note: If you prefer a smooth soup, it can be pureed in a blender.

Reproduced with the kind permission of Kath Leadbeater.

I make a good Soup!

Says '**POTATO PETE**'

By New Year 1946, when food shortages were as bad as at any time during the war, the Dorchester was putting on a less sumptuous feast. Sir Raymond Streat wrote of the News Chronicle's centenary banquet for 425 people, a white tie and tails affair, 'Of course the meal was terrible. A speck of hot lobster; an impossibly tough and exceedingly small leg of chicken; a tiny bit of not very sweet, sweet and a cup of coffee.'

You could eat a tasty and substantial meal for a great deal less than 5s at one of Lyons' Corner Houses or tea shops. Whatever part of the country you were in, this popular chain was reliable and reasonably priced, attracting customers from all classes. The Oxford Street Corner House, one of their many branches in London, remained open throughout the Blitz except for three days in September 1940 when the water supply was cut off.

Lyons' waitresses, known as nippies, wore black dresses with little white aprons and starched white caps. One nippy, Mrs Edith Walsh, worked in the largest of the Brixton teashops in 1941. She arrived for work the morning after an air raid to find that the nearby railway bridge had been hit. Nevertheless they opened up the shop: 'Word soon got round that Lyons' were open and serving food and drink (we had our own generators). It seemed that the world and his wife came into our shop that day. Mrs Hedley (our manageress) told us not to try to keep to our own "stations" just give the people the drinks and food as the counter hands placed it out for us. The teashop was so crowded we couldn't recognise who we'd "put what down for" so we just gave a bill for what we thought was OK. That night we couldn't believe how many bill books we'd used and how much adding up we had to do from the slips at the top. As you can imagine our commission was the best we ever had.'

A glance at the Lyons Soda Fountain tariff takes me back to the post-war days, when my 6d pocket money could still buy a Coffee Nut Sundae, or a fourpenny Peach Sundette with tuppence over for a packet of shortcake biscuits.

Other tea shops and restaurants were less reliable than Lyons. Pam Ashford described lunch at the Grosvenor Tea Rooms, where she was served gooseberry tarts that the waitress assured her were made with real gooseberries. 'Oh my lord! I never tasted anything so foul as those gooseberries in my life. They tasted of mildew, and they tasted of chemicals, and they tasted as if they were unfit for human consumption.'

'Meg and I decide to lunch in Windsor – by the river if possible. In experimental mood we enter a riverside hotel, are ushered into a dim, draped, red and gold dining room, where, in company with young Etonians, ladies with bright hair, officer ATS, Brass Hats, dowagers and pekes, we eat potato soup, fish cake and sauce, chicken hash topped with poached egg, mashed potatoes and greens, and stewed figs

for 6/- each. At our canteen we can get the same quality and a larger quantity of soup, meat, vegetables, sweet, roll and butter, cheese, tea or coffee, for under 2/-. But we enjoyed ourselves. We were paying for the head waiter's white tie, the cunning Hessian drapery and red silk lampshades, the rent and the salaries and all the other exorbitant expense of a select riverside hotel in the shadow of Windsor Castle.' (Maggie Joy Blunt, 25 March 1942).

WILL IT NEVER END?

'I think many people have an idea we are going into another world from today – a world of ease, luxury, plenty. How soon they will come back to earth.'

Kenneth Redmond, 9 May 1945
(the day after VE day)

When Victory in Europe was announced on 8 May 1945, it was clear that there was no prospect of returning to a pre-war world of plenty. On the contrary, 1945 seemed set to be the worst year yet for rationing. Most people realised that the people of Europe were even worse off than the British, and in greater need of food. But weariness had set in, and people who had cheerfully coped with meagre rations for over five years felt they had suffered enough and became dispirited and impatient.

Diarist P.H. Artiss wrote of the world shortage of meat and other staple foods, and of a situation 'worse than at any time during the war... the whole of Europe is now a desert as far as available food stocks are concerned.' At home she found herself having to pay one shilling for a small lettuce, and unable to buy cress at all. '...my husband is quite definitely suffering from poor nutrition today. He NEEDS more milk, butter, cream... I'm terribly worried about him'.

Three months after VE Day, VJ (Victory in Japan) Day was celebrated and the war really had ended. But there was a worsening bread shortage. Muriel Bower in Sheffield wrote, 'Everybody here aren't very thrilled by the news of the latest rationing hit, and also by the prospects of still more tightened belts. We did think that once Japan was beaten we should do away with queues, but it doesn't seem like it. Yesterday I queued a half hour in Woolworth's for some biscuits – and I was under cover. I had to join an immense queue for soapflakes and washing soap too. It was practically as long as the ice cream queue. The fish problem seems to be a bit better here – it isn't quite so rotten although the queues are there still.'

Bread rationing was the last straw for Britain's housewives, and from 1946 even those who throughout the war had regarded rationing as a challenge to be met with cheerful ingenuity, now merely tolerated it with weary resignation. Bread rationing lasted two years, until July 1948. Thereafter a few more foods were 'de-rationed' each year, the last being meat and bacon in June 1954. On 4 July a joyful group of London housewives celebrated in Trafalgar Square by burning a giant ration book.

MARMITE

DEFINITELY DOES YOU GOOD

NOURISHING AND SUSTAINING PURELY VEGETABLE

AND YOU'LL ENJOY IT TOO

Shop Till You Drop

'I've a real love and talent for shopping. I'm stubborn
– I'll not buy things I think are too highly priced, or
queue for them. I firmly believe women are to blame
for high prices. If they would not buy, say, salmon
at 8s 6d a pound, next week it would be cheaper. I'll
order brisket in preference to sirloin, pot-roast it till it's
like chicken, or steam and press it and have good, soft,
butter-like fat for cooking – at half the price of sirloin.'

Nella Last, 7 May 1941

Nella Last with her love of shopping was in a minor-
ity – most women dreaded the drudgery of wartime
shopping. It's difficult to imagine just how different
buying food was in the 1930s and 1940s. Instead of stocking
up weekly at the supermarket, women walked or cycled to
their local high street to call at the butcher, the baker, the
grocer, the fishmonger and the greengrocer. They invariably
had to queue outside each shop for anything up to an hour,
come rain or shine, snow or sleet. And shopping was almost
a daily occurrence; without fridges or freezers, perishable
food that might 'go off' had to be bought in small quantities.

During the war there was an additional incentive
to shop often. You couldn't afford to miss some unexpected bonus. One day the word would go round that the
butcher had some liver; the next day that there had been a
delivery of biscuits at the grocer. The words 'dried apricots'
murmured at an afternoon whist drive would cause a
stampede for the door. Things would vanish from the
shelves within hours and not be seen again for weeks.

People would join a queue simply because it was there,
with no idea what they were queueing for. Josephine
Chalmers, a schoolgirl at the time, remembers her mother
bringing home gelatine after joining a queue. Not knowing
how to use it, she made an inedible jelly, but it made an

SAVE BREAD
and you save lives
SERVE
POTATOES
& you serve the country

shops have an empty and anxious air. Cheese, eggs, onions, oranges, luxury fruits and vegetables are practically unobtainable. Housewives are having to queue for essential foods. We live on potatoes, carrots, sprouts, Swedes, turnips, artichokes and watercress. We are encouraged to use oatmeal to help out the meat ration which was cut at the beginning of the month and now includes all the offal we could once buy without coupons. Cigarettes and sweets are difficult to get though not impossible if one has time and patience to search the shops. Prices are rising. We hear mutterings about inflation and hope that something will be done to prevent it, though how, when we are spending 12 millions a day on our war effort, is hard to imagine.'

For no obvious reason, in some places the shops were still stocked with a pre-war range of goods. Nella Last wrote of a day out to Blackpool in April 1942, 'I cannot *possibly* find words to express my surprise at the lavish luxury of the shops. There was *everything* as in peacetime, and the only restrictions I saw were '7 coupons' or the 'points' value on tinned goods. Tinned fruit, first-grade salmon, whole roast chickens, potted herrings and cooked sausage, plates of attractive salads, fried chicken – all coupon-free. Cakes, pies, biscuits, tarts, gateaux, plate-pies, cream-cakes and fancy cakes. In Woolworth's, Marks and Spencer's, Hill's and Ledgerwood's, *hundreds* of pies and cakes, biscuits, ice cream. Perfumery and cosmetics – lipsticks and *vanishing cream*, rouge and *brilliantine*. Dream hat only 16s11d. 'This season's models – Hollywood styles!'

excellent ball for Josephine to bounce on the kitchen floor.

It was usually women who did the shopping. Men were at the war, or at work, or simply couldn't be trusted. One husband who volunteered to do the shopping came home empty- handed. 'The queues,' he explained, 'were awfully long.'

Today we rarely have to queue except at the supermarket checkout, and most of us load the shopping into the car and drive home. During the war the groceries had to be lugged home on foot. 'When she was older, Mum's right shoulder was much lower than her left. She said she reckoned it was carrying a heavy shopping basket home for all those years,' Gwen Millward explained in a BBC interview.

Diarist Maggie Joy Blunt described the situation in January 1941: 'We are not starving, we are not even underfed, but our usually well-stocked food

And indeed, it seemed that those who could afford to pay could still live well. In Barker's department store in Kensington, London, the food counters were well stocked with poultry and fish, which were unobtainable in poorer areas. Luxury foods such as shellfish, game and even caviar were never rationed and could be obtained throughout the war. Other places were short of just about everything. In Leamington Spa the presence of 10,000 evacuees from Coventry, a city which had suffered terrible bombing, meant there was never enough to go round.

There was little pleasure in queuing except for a sense of achievement in reaching the front of the queue before whatever you were queuing for had run out. But sometimes a camaraderie developed. Women whiled away the time by telling each other what commodities could be got where, and chatting about their families and the progress of the war. However, tempers could become frayed. 'I itched to smack a woman in a shop the other day,' wrote Edie Rutherford, a clerk in the Ministry of Labour, who fought a very personal war on waste. 'The woman behind the counter had turned her back and this customer began to pick up loaf after loaf and feel it, muttering that she often got a stale loaf. I said, "We don't mind how stale the loaf is. We eat till a loaf is done regardless of how long we've had it. And I don't dare to buy bread that has been mauled!" She blushed and said she meant no harm. Maybe she didn't, just another ignorant woman' (Edie Rutherford 12 January 1943).

Queues sometimes started as early as 6am, so it's hardly surprising if people snapped at each other now and then. Sometimes valuable police time was spent controlling queues and making sure that mothers with babies, and the old and infirm, were fairly treated.

IN THE HIGH STREET

In some towns the traditional weekly market continued, but its components were much changed, as Nella Last vividly described. The showy stalls selling biscuits and cheap nasty sweets were gone, and the country women's stalls no longer had eggs, fowls, or butter. There were no 'little glasses of rum butter, golden honey or glowing, homemade orange marmalade, no toffee or candy made on the farm from fresh butter, no glasses of cream or tiny luscious pots of cream cheese.' The fishermen's carts had no flukes or plaice, no pile of sweet 'picked' shrimps or baskets of glistening shelled ones – gun practice in the Bay made it out of bounds. There were only very small, muddy cockles. The 'rows of furry rabbits and strings of sea-birds' that used to hang above the stalls were no longer there.

Today we are used to finding, in Farmers' Markets and Farm Shops, the kind of produce that Nella described, and going to market is a pleasure again. Rabbits and sea birds may be hard to come by, and we may not be too keen to eat them, but we can get farm eggs, poultry, cheeses, fresh vegetables and wild mushrooms.

For most wartime shoppers there was no market available and shopping meant trudging from one high street shop to another.

THE BUTCHER

The housewife's relationship with her butcher was crucial to her family's well-being. You could not shop around, because under the rationing system you had to register with just one supplier, and although the system was designed to ensure that everyone got their fair share of meat, however meagre, there were often shortages and the choice was limited. Most people were used to eating meat at almost every meal and it was a hard habit to break. So a butcher who valued your custom enough to tell you, 'I've got a nice piece of brisket out the back for you,' or, 'I'll be getting salt beef in on Wednesday,' was an important man in your life. It helped if you had the will and the skill to make the most of whatever was available, particularly the cheaper cuts.

SPICED BEEF

Serves 6

My mother's version of this took a week to prepare, turning the meat in the spices daily. But this recipe adapted from Marguerite Patten's *Feeding the Nation*, works very well.

2 teaspoons each of sugar, mustard and salt
4 tablespoons vinegar
1.3–1.8kg (3–4lb) boneless brisket or rolled thin flank
4 bay leaves

8 cloves
1 teaspoon peppercorns
2 onions, peeled and sliced
225g (8oz) carrots, sliced
a handful of chopped parsley

Mix together the sugar, mustard, salt and vinegar and rub them all over the meat. Put the meat in a dish with the bay leaves, cloves and peppercorns and leave for at least 12 hours, turning occasionally.

Put the meat into a casserole or heavy saucepan. Choose one that fits it quite snugly. Add all the spicy juices, the onions, carrots and parsley. Fill with water to just cover the meat, and put the lid on.

Simmer very gently for 3 hours or cook in a very low oven 150°C (300°F) gas mark 2 for 4 hours.

Serve hot, with the liquid thickened to make gravy, or place the meat between two plates with a weight on top until it is cold – this will compress the meat, making it dense and easy to carve.

Once a housewife was on good terms with the butcher, she could make her order over the telephone and trust him to deliver good quality meat. It would be delivered, wrapped in brown paper, by a boy on a bicycle with a big wicker basket attached to the handlebars. Errand boys no longer exist, but in those days they were part of any street scene, sometimes showing off by riding with no hands, and invariably whistling the current hit tune. A typical delivery for a household of two might consist of a couple of lamb chops, a few pence worth of corned beef, a good jelly bone for making stock, a few ounces of suet to make pastry for pies, and ½lb of sausages.

Sausages were sometimes unobtainable. In January 1941 Pam Ashford wrote '… there were no sausages in Hyndland last week. (We associate this with the meat scarcity rather than the machine-gunning of Waddell's sausage factory.) I promised to keep my eyes skinned down town.' Later in the same week the newspapers reported that sausages were likely to disappear altogether. Even when they were available the meat content was often almost non-existent. People bought them when not much else was available.

Like sausages, offal was not rationed, therefore much in demand, and scarce. People would buy the parts of animals that were previously thrown away, like ox-cheek, pigs' trotters and cow heel. Most people drew the line at sheep's head but 'If I got some liver I ran home as happy as if I had won a fortune', one woman remembers.

Today we are unlikely to cook these items, partly because few butchers sell them and partly because we are a touch squeamish.

KIDNEYS IN RED WINE

Serves 4

There are many delicious ways to cook kidneys and liver, and they could be eaten far more often than they are. Calves' livers and lambs' kidneys are the most delicate in texture and flavour, but they are also the most expensive. Pigs' livers and kidneys are a good economical alternative. If you use a pig's kidney, slice it thinly rather than halving it.

12 lamb kidneys, skinned
1 tablespoon plain flour
salt and freshly ground black
  pepper
55g (2oz) butter
1 onion, peeled and sliced

140g (5oz) mushrooms,
  washed and sliced
2 tomatoes, skinned and
  chopped
150ml (5fl oz) red wine
1 tablespoon chopped parsley

Preheat the oven to 180°C (350°F) gas mark 4.

Cut out and discard the core from each kidney and cut the kidneys in half lengthways. Season the flour and roll the kidney halves in it to coat them.

Heat the butter and gently fry the onion until transparent. Transfer to an ovenproof dish. Turn up the heat a little and brown the kidneys on both sides. Add the mushrooms and cook for 2 minutes. Add the tomatoes and red wine and stir all together.

Transfer to the ovenproof dish, cover with foil and bake in the preheated oven for 25 minutes.

Sprinkle with the parsley and serve with rice or mashed potato as preferred.

Variation: Leave out the tomatoes and use white wine or sherry and finish with a few spoonfuls of cream with a teaspoon of wholegrain mustard stirred in.

Go easy with **BREAD**

eat **POTATOES** instead

THE BAKER

'Remember that if everyone in Great Britain wasted ½oz bread daily we should be wasting 250,000 tons of wheat a year, and that 30 wheat ships would be required to carry that amount' (Lord Woolton).

In spite of government policy to grow as much as possible at home, it was still necessary to import large quantities of wheat to make enough of the despised National Loaf to feed the nation. In an effort to reduce imports, and therefore the number of cargo ships at risk from enemy attack, Lord Woolton waged war on wasting bread, and urged people to eat potatoes instead.

The anti-waste campaign was supported by legal measures, and these were not idle threats. A Miss Mary Bridget O'Sullivan of Barnet, Hertfordshire was fined ten pounds with two guineas costs for wasting bread. She had asked her maid, who paid a lesser fine of five shillings, to put stale bread out to feed the birds in the garden. Since hearing her story I have been conscience-stricken about wasting bread. Now, when the heel of a loaf is left over, I whiz it up in the blender before it grows stale and freeze the crumbs for a future gratin topping or apple charlotte.

Gwen Millward remembers relieving her mother of part of the shopping burden. 'I used to walk home from school every dinner time, and my mother gave me three jobs to do each day. That's how I earned my pocket money. First of all I had to go to Miss Stokes bread shop, which was just around the corner in Warwick Place. I always bought a large tin loaf price fourpence halfpenny.

When I came back from the bread shop, my mother gave me the household scraps to take to the communal pig bin.'

Bread was the one food people could not bear to be without and when, soon after the end of the war, it was in short supply and not always obtainable, people were upset. When, finally, it was rationed for the first time in 1946 they were incensed, and when white bread finally appeared again in the 1950s they were overjoyed.

THE GROCER

'Go carefully with the tin opener' (Lord Woolton). The Minister of Food's exhortation to keep tinned food in reserve, as iron rations, was largely ignored. Few rumours on the bush telegraph had so many women hurrying to the grocer as news that a consignment of tinned soup, fruit or salmon had arrived. Heinz's and Crosse & Blackwell's soups (vegetable, chicken, celery, vegetable and kidney) were much in demand, although some customers thought the standard had declined since the war started. 'One day the kidney soup made me vomit,' said one woman.

You had to act quickly to get anything unusual that was off the ration. A customer lured into a Glasgow store by the sight of a tin of Heinz oxtail soup, was thrilled to spot a box of dried peaches, not visible from the door. 'I doubted my eyes so much that I had to ask the assistant what was in the box. Mrs Muir went around 12.30 and they were gone then.'

BREAD AND CHEESE PUDDING

Serves 2 as a starter or 4 as a main course

A delicious, nutritious mixture of cheese, bread, eggs and milk, like a soufflé. During rationing a passable version could have been made with dried milk and dried eggs but it would use up 2 people's cheese ration for a fortnight.

250g (9oz) fresh white breadcrumbs
280g (10oz) grated mature Cheddar cheese
600ml (1pt) milk

55g (2oz) butter
4 eggs
salt and freshly ground black pepper
1 teaspoon English mustard

Preheat the oven to 200°C (400°F) gas mark 6. Grease a 20cm/8in soufflé dish.

Mix the breadcrumbs and cheese in a bowl.

In a saucepan, heat the milk and butter until the butter melts; pour it over the breadcrumbs and stir.

Whisk the eggs with the salt, pepper and mustard. Stir them into the breadcrumb mixture, and pour into the prepared dish. Leave to stand for 1 hour.

Bake the pudding in the preheated oven for about 40 minutes until risen and golden. Serve warm.

From *The Dictionary of Daily Wants 1859*

PINEAPPLE
UPSIDE-DOWN CAKE

Serves 4–6

More of a pudding than a cake. Make it in an old-fashioned cake tin – the juice would leak out of a modern one with a removable base. Or use a soufflé dish. Serve it either hot or cold, with custard or cream.

2 tablespoons brown sugar
100g (3½ oz) butter, plus
   extra for greasing
425g (15oz) tinned pineapple
   rings

125g (4½ oz) self-raising flour
100g (3½ oz) sugar
1 egg
100ml (3½ fl oz) milk

Preheat the oven to 180°C (350°F) gas mark 4. Grease an 18cm/7in cake tin or soufflé dish.

In a saucepan, gently melt the brown sugar, half of the butter and 3 tablespoons of juice from the pineapple tin. Boil the mixture until it becomes a thick golden brown syrup. Pour the syrup over the base of the cake tin.

Arrange the pineapple rings on the syrup in two layers, cutting the rings if necessary, to cover the base.

Sift the flour and mix it with the sugar.

Melt the remaining butter, then beat it into the flour along with the egg and milk. You could use a hand-held electric whisk to do this. Stop once the mixture is smooth, it's important not to over-mix the batter. Pour the mixture over the pineapple and bake in the preheated oven for about 40 minutes.

Turn it out on to a plate, pineapple slices uppermost, and serve.

Variation: Other fruit such as apples, plums or apricots can be used in the same way.

Besides being purveyors of hard-to-come-by, off-the-ration tinned food and occasional treats like Kia-Ora orange squash and chocolate biscuits, grocers were responsible for selling each family their ration of bacon, cheese, sugar, tea and eggs. Butter, margarine and cooking fat were also important parts of the weekly ration.

When people first realised they would have to cook with margarine instead of butter, and perhaps even spread it on their bread, they were deeply suspicious. Margarine was thought to cause stomach upsets, but to be just about palatable if melted and mixed with butter.

The shortage of eggs was also hard to bear. Before the war everyone had eaten on average three eggs a week. In 1940 millions of hens were slaughtered to reduce imports of feeding stuffs, and many grocers found it impossible to get enough eggs for their customers. A young mum living in Cornwall wrote: 'The egg difficulty persists. Occasionally the United Dairy allows me three in a week. I asked the milkman if he had any this morning. He shook his head and said, "I haven't any today, but they have given me a pamphlet to explain to the customers why we haven't got any." "I can't give that to the baby for her dinner," I said.'

The problem was alleviated in June 1942 when packets of dried eggs from America began to appear on the grocers' shelves. People disliked them at first and the Ministry of Food issued a little lecture pointing out how much shipping space was saved by dried eggs: 'Shell eggs are five-sixths water: Why import water?'

THE GREENGROCER

'My cupboard might as well be bare.
Bereft, I wander everywhere
And try, nose in the empty air,
To sniff a whiff of onion.'

Anonymous

It's hard to imagine cooking for more than a few days without using onions, but early in the war, owing to the loss of supplies from the Channel Islands and Britanny, onions disappeared from the shops. It was not until the end of the war that the familiar Breton Onion Man reappeared, wearing his beret and riding a bicycle festooned with neatly tied ropes of onions.

The lack of onions was a serious blow to housewives struggling to make cheaper cuts of meat palatable or to invent tasty meatless dishes. You

tended to do rather well out of presents from grateful patients and one said that the best present he ever received was a large Spanish onion.

From time to time there were shortages of other fruit and vegetables. For a while peas were almost unobtainable, and at one London greengrocer when the word went round that he would have cooking apples in the shop, a queue starting at 6am the following morning. It was a mile long and he sold one apple to each customer until they had all gone. At another London shop a woman queued for three hours for the prize of three apples *or* a pound of rhubarb. Luxury fruit was sometimes available for very high prices, a melon in August 1941 for £2, for example, and grapes at 17s 6d a pound.

One commodity was never in short supply. The Ministry was always keen to promote carrots, and although they may not really help you see in the blackout, they are undoubtedly very good for you. But carrot flan? Carrot jam? Or curried carrots or carrot fudge? No thank you. But Carrot Cake is another matter, and has become a deservedly popular classic.

cannot make a full-flavoured soup or stock without an onion, or a stew or a savoury pie. In 1941 people were desperate to get their hands on one. In February that year a one-and-a-half pound onion was raffled among the staff of the *Times* and raised £4 3s 4d. In March, at a first aid lecture, when one woman remarked that she did not cry if she wore her gas mask when peeling onions, all the women present yelled, 'Where did you get the onions?' Doctors

CHEESY LEEK AND POTATO GRATIN

Serves 4

A lovely supper dish eaten just as it is or with a few crispy rashers of streaky bacon, a luxury that was sadly rationed to wartime cooks from January 1940.

55g (2oz) butter, plus extra
for greasing
3 leeks, cleaned and thinly
sliced
1kg (2lb 4oz) potatoes, peeled
and thinly sliced

salt and freshly ground black
pepper
225g (8oz) Cheddar cheese,
grated

Preheat the oven to 190°C (375°F) gas mark 5.

Gently melt the butter in a saucepan, then add the leeks and cook until they start to soften.

Grease a baking dish with a little extra butter. Layer one quarter of the sliced potatoes at the bottom of the dish.

Spread half the leeks over the potatoes and season with salt and pepper. Add another layer of potato, then half the Cheddar cheese. Repeat the four layers, then cover the dish with foil and bake in the preheated oven for 30 minutes.

Uncover and continue baking for another 20–30 minutes until the potato is soft when pierced with a knife, and brown on top.

COURGETTE SOUFFLÉ

Serves 3–4

Courgettes can be sliced or grated for a gratin, roast around the Sunday joint or puréed to make a creamy soup. One of the most delicious ways to cook them is in a soufflé. The following recipe is adapted from one that appears in Elizabeth David's *French Provincial Cooking*.

2 tablespoons olive oil
1 garlic clove, peeled and
  finely chopped
500g (1lb 2oz) small
  courgettes, finely sliced
55g (2oz) butter, plus extra
  for greasing

55g (2oz) plain flour
250ml (9fl oz) milk
4 eggs separated into 3 yolks
  and 4 whites
55g (2oz) Cheddar or Gruyère
  cheese, grated
freshly ground black pepper

Preheat the oven to 180°C (350°F) gas mark 4 and grease a soufflé dish with butter.

Over a low heat, gently heat the oil in a large saucepan and add the garlic and courgettes. Stir frequently to prevent them sticking to the pan and so they soften without browning. Cook for about 20 minutes, until they are completely soft and almost all their water has evaporated.

Remove from the heat and beat with a wooden spoon to make a fairly smooth purée.

Melt the butter in a small saucepan set over a low heat then stir in the flour. Cook for 1 minute, then add the milk. Simmer for 1–2 minutes, stirring well, until it transforms into a thick, smooth sauce.

Tip the sauce onto the courgettes. Beat in the egg yolks and the cheese. Season to taste with black pepper.

CARROT CAKE –
HOMAGE TO DOCTOR CARROT

Serves 12

What a pity British wartime cooks seem not to have known about carrot cake. It would have cheered them up so much. The nearest thing I have found in wartime recipe books is a recipe for carrot buns – good, but not as sticky-crumbly as the cake. Use a hot spoon to measure the syrup.

4 eggs
150g (5½ oz) soft brown sugar
2 tablespoons golden syrup
300ml (10½ fl oz) sunflower oil
300g (10½ oz) wholemeal
   self-raising flour
½ teaspoon salt
1 teaspoon cinnamon
1 teaspoon ground ginger
½ teaspoon nutmeg

½ teaspoon bicarbonate of soda
350g (12oz) carrots, peeled and
   finely grated

For the cream cheese icing:
200g (7oz) cream cheese
55g (2oz) softened unsalted butter
2oz (2oz) sifted icing sugar
1 teaspoon vanilla essence

Preheat the oven to 180°C (350°F) gas mark 4. Grease a 23cm (9in) cake tin and line the base with baking paper.

In a large bowl beat the eggs, sugar and syrup with a hand-held electric whisk until the mixture is pale and thick. Add the oil and beat for a few more minutes.

Mix the flour, salt, spices and bicarbonate of soda and sift them into the mixture. Tip the bran bits left in the sieve into the mixture and fold it all together. Fold in the grated carrot and put the mixture into the prepared tin.

Bake in the preheated oven for 45–50 minutes, until a thin skewer inserted in the centre comes out clean.

Leave to cool slightly in the tin before turning out onto a wire rack to cool completely.

Beat all the cream cheese icing ingredients together until smooth, then spread over the cake when it is cold.

Occasionally shopkeepers suffered from bureaucracy gone mad. All food supplies were controlled by the Ministry of Food, and one day an unfortunate man who had just inherited a greengrocer's shop in a tiny Scottish village received a telephone call from the man from the Ministry. Under the points system, he was told, 600 tins of meat would be delivered to him, which he must accept whether he wanted them or not.

THE FISHMONGER
There were always queues for fish, sometimes lasting hours. Such a queue yielded, for one family whose cupboard was bare, herrings for lunch, shrimps for tea and kippers for breakfast. Kippers were considered very acceptable birthday or Christmas presents. The more familiar cod and haddock were in short supply, and anyone hoping fish would prove a cheap and plentiful alternative to meat was disappointed. The Government did promote 'fresh-salted' cod from Iceland at 9d a pound but fishmongers were reluctant to stock it as they had to soak it to de-salt it before selling it, and the controlled price reduced their profit margin. By comparison, haddock cost an astronomical 4s per pound. Those fish that were affordable were 'not attractive fish like plaice or sole – but lumps of "fish flesh" that might be a whale cut into 1lb bits.'

Traditionally, British people have always been unadventurous about fish, to put it mildly. What they really liked was tinned salmon, with cod and haddock a close second. Most wartime cookery books are equally unadventurous, simply referring to 'white fish'

and occasionally offering a recipe for mackerel or herring. Anything new was regarded with suspicion. Fresh tunny (tuna) was sometimes on offer, caught in the 1930s and 1940s off the north-east coast of Britain but there were few takers. As for Snoek, the dark-fleshed fish introduced by John Strachey when he was Minister of Food, the British people were having none of it, though I'm told by someone who has eaten it in South Africa that it's perfectly palatable. No doubt they would be equally resistant to pollack, gurnard and other fish that we eat now that worldwide stocks of cod and haddock are dangerously low.

MY VERY GOOD FRIEND, THE MILKMAN

Milk came in glass bottles, left by the milkman on the doorstep. From December 1941 it was allocated to 3 pints per person per week. Occasionally this was reduced to 2 pints a week, while young children, expectant mothers and invalids were each allowed a pint a day. Free school milk was introduced in August 1946. At my school it was served at mid-morning break, in special bottles which held a third of a pint, with silver foil tops through which you could push a straw. It was thin and tepid and sometimes in summer it was slightly off. One diarist remembers a winter when the milk froze in the bottles and the teacher put it on the classroom stove to thaw.

Tinned condensed milk, sweet and thick, was sometimes available on points, and you could sometimes get dried milk, which was fine to cook with. If you had dried eggs and dried milk in the larder, you only needed flour and water to make pancakes.

GRANNY LASCELLES' FUDGE SAUCE

Serves 6

This is too solid to be called a sauce; my grandmother used to give it to us with vanilla ice cream after Sunday lunch.

Put an unopened tin of sweetened condensed milk in a saucepan and cover it with water. Boil it for 3 hours. When it has cooled, open the tin and spoon out the toffee-like sauce.

THE BLACK MARKET

It was against the law to sell food without coupons or with forged coupons, food stolen in transit, meat illicitly slaughtered, or food produced at home. Fines could be imposed up to £500 with or without two years' imprisonment plus three times the value of the goods. Approximately 900 inspectors were employed by the Ministry of Food to make sure retailers, wholesalers and customers abided by the rules. They found that most food sold on the black market came from farmers and smallholders.

Almost any produce could be obtained if you knew whom to ask and could afford to pay a premium. A London butcher supplied his customers with black-market meat for a tip of two shillings and sixpence, and there was no shortage of takers. People would leave out tips for the milkman in the empty bottles to be sure of getting extra milk albeit at a premium price.

There were also numerous amateur black marketers, like the woman in a block of flats in Sheffield who used to sell the orange juice she got from the clinic for her baby. Diaries and memoirs provide plenty of other examples. Joy Eldridge wrote, 'Dad's friend the chef helped us out but it was a costly affair, but we, like everyone else did what they had to do to survive, some called it "black market," we called it keeping body and soul together.'

'Scandalous prices are asked and paid for drinks,' Maggie Joy Blunt complained, 'Cherry brandy 2s 9d a glass. Nearly all the stuff is black market. Publicans cannot get legitimate stock, demand is great and people pay what is asked. On Boxing Night one round cost one man 15s. Some men spend as much as £10 in one evening.'

Most people knew someone who knew someone who made use of the black market from time to time. Even the clergy were involved; a Methodist minister was said to deal regularly in eggs and to have a source of silk stockings and marmalade. On one occasion the Bishop of Bradford and a colleague were overheard discussing how to share out a 40lb ham they had acquired.

A boarding house landlady was surprised and shocked by four people who arrived from Glasgow with seven double loin chops and four eggs that she cooked for their tea. The next morning they produced four large fillet steaks for breakfast and a 4lb joint of beef for dinner. The following day, seven more double loin chops, four eggs and a large steak and kidney pie. And so it went on. She had been unable to get meat for a week, but one of the four guests told her he just went into the shop and 'talked to the butcher'. No coupons were involved.

UNDER THE COUNTER

People buying for boarding houses could usually get things not otherwise available, like tinned milk, fruit, salmon, chicken soup and tomato soup. A grocer explained, 'We have privileged customers to whom we grant privileges that we are not prepared to grant to ordinary customers.' There was nothing illegal about this, as none of these items was rationed.

'Under the counter' was a recognised system for canny shoppers. Shopkeepers who valued their regular customers would gladly put aside for them anything that was in short supply, and give them precedence over casual shoppers. But it had to be done discreetly. Pam Ashford described in her daryhow a friend used

to buy eggs at a small dairy.

When the supply dried up she asked the owner, 'Why can I never get any eggs?'

'It's your own fault,' he replied. 'You always ask me when I have a shopful of customers.'

'There's no one else in the shop now,' she pointed out.

'Go and look out of the door and see if there is anyone in the street' he said.

She did so and reported that the coast was clear. He promptly produced three eggs.

MAKING ENDS MEET

Today we still need to be as flexible in our shopping as wartime housewives became, and apply the same principles of common sense and thrift. The reward is satisfaction from buying fresh fruit and vegetables, locally sourced if possible, and varying our menus with the changing seasons. Flexible shopping means looking for unusual ingredients at the butcher, the baker and the deli, and learning how to cook them.

The difference is that today we don't suffer from rationing or scarcities. It's a lot more fun for us to do the rounds of the stalls at the farmers' market or chat to our regular butcher about the best way make an oxtail stew or what to do with pig trotters. Local shops may not be able to compete with supermarket prices, but the small extra cost can be offset by saving on fuel costs. And it's impossible to put a value on the good relationship regular customers can establish with their suppliers.

WAR-TIME COOKERY

By
HILDA M.K. NIELD

New Edition

9d.

Putting Food on the Table

Mass Observation diaries from 1939 give a good idea of what people ate before rationing began. In February of that year Christopher Tomlin, a salesman in his twenties living with his parents in Preston, was invited to dinner with his two aunts. They gave him roast pork with sage and onion stuffing, apple sauce, mashed potatoes and greens, followed by fruit (cooked, presumably) and Devonshire cream. They drank sherry and a bottle of pale ale each. Not much sign of deprivation in his aunts' house. At home, however, his mother was already finding that cakes were scarce in the shops, and had taken to baking her own rock buns, Bakewell tarts, and egg and bacon tarts.

A few months later Maggie Joy Blunt, who lived alone, found the current food supply good. She had plenty of wholemeal bread that she spread with mixed butter and marge, fresh green vegetables and salads from the garden, and marmalade, figs, sultanas, prunes and honey in the larder. Fresh fruit was expensive but English apples and plums were just coming in.

A typical meal for Maggie Joy was half a steamed mackerel (3d), new potatoes (2d or 3d a pound), garden spinach, parsley sauce made from lard, wholemeal flour, water and home-grown parsley (this sauce can't have been very delicious), followed by stewed fruit with bread and butter.

By the middle of 1940 the full effect of rationing was being felt, and people were short of time as well as food. 'There is no economic base to our housekeeping', wrote Pam Ashford 'and everything is on labour-saving lines. We have only one course at lunch, with coffee and fancy biscuits to follow. Supper: biscuits and cheese; Charlie [her brother] breakfasts off Butterette biscuits; my Saturday lunch consists of Healthy Life biscuits

EGG AND BACON TART

Serves 4

A more frugal version of this recipe would use milk instead of cream, and potato pastry, made by substituting grated raw potato for some of the flour (see the Mock Apricot Flan, page 148). I have tried this and the pastry is, perhaps surprisingly, crisp and short and doesn't taste of potato.

300g (10½ oz) shortcrust pastry
1 tablespoon olive oil
150g (5½ oz) smoked bacon
 rashers, chopped
1 onion, peeled and chopped

300ml (10½ fl oz) double cream
3 eggs, beaten
4 whole eggs
salt and freshly ground black pepper

Preheat the oven to 180°C (350°F) gas mark 4.

Line a 20cm (8in) tart tin with the pastry. Cover with baking paper, fill with baking beans and bake blind in the preheated oven for about 15 minutes until pale gold.

Remove the paper and beans and bake for a further 5 minutes to dry out.

Meanwhile heat the oil in a frying pan and add the bacon and onion. Fry for about 5 minutes until the onion is soft and the bacon crisp. Spoon the mixture into the pastry-lined tart tin.

Add the cream to the beaten eggs, season with salt and pepper and pour over the bacon. Crack the four whole eggs into the mixture and bake for 20 minutes until cooked through.

nibbled in the darkness of the cinema.'

Maggie Joy Blunt was still benefiting from her garden, and recorded lunching off vegetable stew and French beans with a thick Parmesan sauce, followed by a steamed pudding made from rhubarb and bread. She had taken to eating cold boiled rice for breakfast and rice again for lunch, with salad, which she deemed a success.

As the war continued and rationing got worse, her meals became more and more eccentric: 'Tonight ate cheese thinly sliced and cooked in margarine with tomatoes and milk, followed by raw cabbage, celery and apple salad and a pud made from stale scone and some vile ABC jam sponge cake soaked in prune juice, mixed with plenty of home-made plum jam and steamed. The plum jam going mouldy – other people's home-made jam too, perhaps because beet, not cane sugar'. Unappetising perhaps, but nutritionally speaking, exemplary.

THE MOTHER OF INVENTION

Cooks became expert at adapting recipes to the available ingredients. Nella Last was proud of 'one of the best puddings I've made for a long time.' She used suet from a kidney bought from the butcher, two slices of wholemeal bread, and candied peel made by boiling orange peel in a little honey and water. To make one egg do the work of two, she beat it in hot water. The other ingredients were a 5½oz pot of sweetened bun flour and a tablespoon of sultanas. 'It made a very generous helping for the three of us,' Nella wrote, 'a helping for my husband to have tomorrow, and enough for a small portion each on Friday. No milk to make sauce so made custard with water, and honey to sweeten.'

Nella, knowing that her husband (like most men, I suspect) didn't care for economy dishes, told him she'd made honey sauce for a change. 'By Gad its grand – brings out the real flavour of the pudding', was his comment. On another occasion she tried him with a cocoa-carrot-flour and bread-crust-and-bit-of kidney fat pudding, again without revealing the ingredients. It too went down well.

Other housewives were less inventive. When they had used up their meat ration they would often serve baked potatoes with brown sauce or bread soaked in Oxo as main dishes. A packed lunch to take to work consisted of sandwiches filled with potato crisps. A Croydon housewife had a success with MI5 Pudding, so called because she refused to disclose the ingredients. They were, in fact, liver, sausage meat and onion. Her children thought it super.

When milk was readily available, people would supplement the meagre butter ration by skimming the cream off the top, putting it into a glass jar or wide-topped bottle, and taking turns to shake it vigorously. Eventually the cream separated, yielding a small nugget of butter and a lot of buttermilk which could be used in cakes and pancakes. It works. My grandchildren have made butter in this way.

Cakes, pies and tarts, always a key part of British cooking, were much missed. The combined ration of butter, margarine and cooking fat was seldom enough for a regular baking session, and women would go to any lengths to supplement it. When tins of ham, corned beef or minced pork were opened, the fat surrounding the meat would be scraped away and used to make pastry. Liquid paraffin, a strong laxative, was a surprisingly successful substitute for other fats until the Government issued an instruction that it was only to be used for medicinal purposes. Then a few desperate cake-makers turned to the children's cod liver oil.

Dried elderberries and chopped prunes were substituted for currants in cakes and puddings, and one woman successfully tried wine gums, though they tended to sink to the bottom of the dish. Even hideous mistakes like a cake flavoured with Dettol stored in a bottle labelled 'almond essence' were not wasted, but consumed to the last crumb.

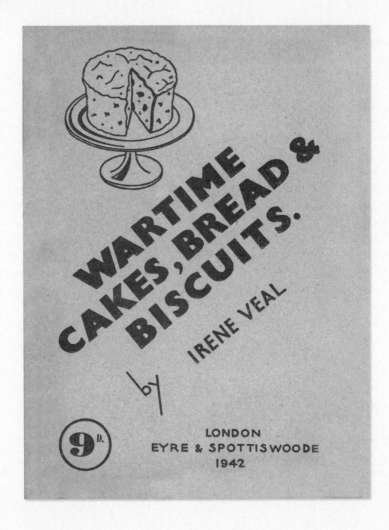

FAT-FREE SPONGE CAKE

Serves 8–10

A good recipe then if you had used up your fat ration and could get the eggs, and good now for anyone on a dairy-free diet.

3 large eggs, separated
225g (8oz) caster sugar
80ml (2½ fl oz) warm water
1 teaspoon vanilla essence

1 teaspoon baking powder
140g (5oz) plain white flour
butter or oil, to grease tins

Preheat the oven to 190°C (375°F) gas mark 5. Grease two 20cm (8in) sandwich cake tins and line with baking paper.

Put the egg yolks and sugar in a large bowl. Beat with an electric whisk for 2 minutes.

Add the warm water and vanilla and continue whisking for 10 minutes until the mixture is mousse-like.

Add the baking powder to the flour and sieve into the egg mixture a few tablespoons at a time, folding it in gently.

In a separate bowl, whisk the egg whites until they hold firm peaks, then fold gently into the mixture. Divide between the two tins and bake in the preheated oven for 20 minutes.

Turn the cakes out immediately on to a wire rack. Allow to cool completely before sandwiching them together with jam or fruit (sliced or purée) with or without whipped cream or low-fat fromage frais.

your NATIONAL WHEATMEAL BREAD *is here!*

WHOLEMEAL BREAD

Makes 2 loaves

'**We must think of ways and means of making bread when our emergency supply is exhausted or white bread is rationed or unobtainable and replaced by a wholemeal bread which although not so appetising in appearance is a more valuable food,'** wrote the Vicomte de Mauduit in *They Can't Ration These*. This recipe is adapted from the Vicomte's.

1 ½ lb wholemeal bread flour	1 dessertspoon of honey or
1 ½ tablespoons salt	treacle
1 ½ teaspoons dried yeast	450 ml tepid water

Preheat the oven to 200°C (400°F) gas mark 6.

In a large bowl mix the flour, salt and yeast together. Dissolve the honey or treacle in the water. Make a well in the centre of the flour mixture and pour in the water. Mix with a fork and then with your hands and knead until a uniform dough is formed.

Put the dough in the bowl, cover with a damp cloth and a plastic sheet to stop the cloth drying out. Leave in a warm place such as an airing cupboard or on the shelf above a radiator until the dough has doubled in size, usually about 2 hours.

Turn the dough out on to a floured surface, and knead with floured hands. Cut the dough into two pieces and put each into a 1.5litre loaf tin or (says the Vicomte) an ordinary garden flowerpot. Cover with the damp cloth and plastic and leave to rise for another 2 hours.

Bake in the preheated oven for about 30 minutes (check after 20 mins to make sure the crust is not burning).

To test the loaves, turn them out of the tins (easy) or flowerpots (difficult) and tap with your knuckles. If they sound hollow they are done. Leave the loaves to cool on a wire rack.

SHEER MONOTONY

The Radio Doctor understood the importance of variety in a healthy diet. 'Scientifically speaking,' he said, 'you could live only on milk and potatoes and cheese and something green and raw, and be healthy. As a matter of fact you would be bored to death and your digestion would suffer.'

Those who had taken up Digging for Victory with enthusiasm found it comparatively easy to produce varied, healthy and tasty meals. Kathleen Tipper wrote, 'As we were having tea today my father remarked that the table did not look like the table of a country in the fourth year of war, so I noted down what we were having. Spam, cheese, tomatoes, celery, beetroot, pickled onions and two sorts of home-made chutney,

Swiss roll and apples.... Everything on our table except the Spam and cheese and Swiss roll came from the garden...'

But those who were forced into a more monotonous diet found the sameness of meal after meal depressing.' How I grow sick of never-ending starch – bread, bread, bread', wrote one diarist. Another complained, 'Toad-in-the-hole is *not* what it was. That lovely pork sausage in a yellow batter, shining with fat, has given place to a beef beast, flavourless and rough-skinned, in a heavy khaki batter made with milk powder.'

One way to relieve the monotony of a restricted range of food is to ring the changes with herbs and spices, but this seems to have been only half-heartedly attempted during the war. Apart from a sprinkling of parsley as a garnish with almost everything, and curried almost-anything, the opportunity was missed. Garlic, in almost daily use in many kitchens today, was unknown.

Good Eating: Suggestions for Wartime Dishes compiled by the *Daily Telegraph* was in advance of its time, with a chapter entitled the Art of Flavouring, which recommended growing, drying and blending various herbs. But they were conspicuous by their absence in the actual recipes, which mostly came from *Daily Telegraph* readers.

HERBS

Herbs bought or picked fresh and then frozen have far better flavour than dusty dried herbs bought in a packet. Traditional herbs that no wartime cook would have managed without and neither would we, are thyme to combine with lemon for a roast chicken, sage for pork and goose, parsley for parsley sauce to eat with ham or gammon, and mint for peas and new potatoes. Add a bay leaf and some garlic to thyme and parsley, and you have a bouquet garni, essential to flavour stock, soups and stews. To these basics, modern cooks would add tarragon as a partner for fish and chicken, rosemary with lamb, and chives to snip into omelettes or to garnish soups. The following herbs are those I would consider essential for the garden, windowsill, freezer or store cupboard:

Herbs

BAY

BASIL

CHIVES

GARLIC

MARJORAM

MINT

PARSLEY

ROSEMARY

SAGE

TARRAGON

THYME

SPICES

My grandmother's cupboard contained little glass bottles of vanilla essence, almond essence, peppermint oil and cochineal to colour cake mixtures and icing bright pink.

There were also cloves for apple pies and to stick into onions to flavour the milk for bread sauce. Packets of nutmeg, ginger and allspice gathered dust until 'stir-up Sunday' came round and it was time to make the Christmas pudding. Nowadays we are much more liberal with spices in both sweet and savoury dishes, and most home cooks will use the following:

Spices

BLACK PEPPERCORNS

CAYENNE PEPPER

CHILLI POWDER

CINNAMON

CLOVES

CORIANDER

CUMIN

CURRY POWDER OR PASTE

GINGER ROOT
(plus a jar of preserved ginger in syrup)

NUTMEG

PAPRIKA

TURMERIC

VANILLA (keep a pod in a jar of sugar)

DRIED EGGS

'Hey! Little hen! When, when, when will you lay me an egg for my tea?
Hey! Little hen! When, when, when will you try to supply one for me?
Get into your nest, do your little best. Get it off your chest. I can do the rest.
Hey! Little hen! When, when, when, will you lay me an egg for my tea?'

A popular wartime song by Ralph Butler and Noel Gay

At the beginning of the war vast numbers of hens were slaughtered to save on imported chicken feed, so eggs became very scarce. From June 1941 the ration was one fresh egg a week, but this was often reduced to one every two weeks. However, expectant mothers and children were allowed up to eighteen eggs each per month. Family members would hover round the toddler's high chair waiting for him to reject his boiled egg. Householders with backyard hens became very popular, and were courted by anyone with goods to barter.

From June 1942 the situation was relieved by the import of dried egg powder from the USA. A packet containing the equivalent of 12 eggs cost 1s 9d. The Ministry of Food urged people to buy them: 'The motto for eggs is, dry, dry and dry again.'

Fresh eggs in their shells were often so stale that housewives became reconciled to dried eggs in their drab cardboard boxes, although some said that dried egg itself tasted of cardboard.

Eggs have always been a great standby, particularly when meat is not readily available. Obviously you couldn't boil or poach dried egg, but they could be scrambled, and made a passable omelette. They also meant women could make cakes and puddings again, which gave morale a big boost. Some dishes, pancakes for example, were made almost entirely of dried eggs mixed with dried milk.

"DRIED EGGS
are <u>my</u> eggs —
my <u>whole</u> eggs
and
<u>nothing but</u> my eggs"

Dried eggs are the complete hen's eggs, both the white and the yolk, dried to a powder. Nothing is added. Nothing but moisture and the shell taken away, leaving the eggs themselves as wholesome, as digestible and as full of nourishment and health-protecting value as if you had just taken the eggs new laid from the nest. So put the eggs back into your breakfast menus. And what about a big, creamy omelette for supper? You can have it savoury; or sweet, now that you get extra jam.

DRIED EGGS build you up!

In war-time, the most difficult foods for us to get are the body-builders. Dried eggs build muscle and repair tissue in just the same way as do chops and steaks; and are better for health-protection. So we are particularly lucky to be able to get dried eggs to make up for any shortage of other body-builders such as meat, fish, cheese, milk.

Your allowance of DRIED EGG is equal to 3 eggs a week

You can now get one 12-egg packet (price 1/3) per 4-week rationing period — three fine fresh eggs a week, at the astonishingly low price of

1¼d. each. Children (holders of green ration books) get two packets each rationing period. You buy your dried eggs at the shop where you are registered for shell eggs; poultry keepers can buy anywhere.
Don't hoard your dried eggs; use them up — there are plenty more coming!

Note. *Don't make up dried eggs until you are ready to use them; they should not be allowed to stand after they've been mixed with water or other liquid. Use dry when making cakes and so on, and add a little more moisture when mixing.*

FREE — DRIED EGG LEAFLET containing many interesting recipes, will be sent on receipt of a postcard addressed to Dept. 627E, Food Advice Service, Ministry of Food, London, W.1.

ISSUED BY THE MINISTRY OF FOOD (S.74)

MOCK FOOD

Women went to great lengths to relieve the monotony of rationed food and satisfy their longing for pre-war treats. When the real thing was not available, they found a way of simulating it. The main ingredients of Mock Crab were tomatoes and cheese. Mock Salmon, strangely enough, had almost identical ingredients but with the addition of breadcrumbs. No fish had been near either recipe. An entirely meat-free Mock Goose was made from potatoes, apples, peas, cheese and dried sage. Probably it was the sage that reminded the gullible of Roast Goose. A recipe for Mock Grouse, made by stuffing a pigeon with a kipper, cannot have been serious.

If you forget that these mock recipes are imitations of something else, some of them are rather good.

MOCK DUCK
(SAUSAGE & APPLE MEAT LOAF)

Serves 4

In wartime when there was very little meat in sausages, this would have been almost a vegetarian dish. Today you can buy sausage meat with a high pork content, or skin some good quality sausages to get a better result. Does it taste like duck? No. Does it look like duck? No. Calling it 'Mock Duck' must have satisfied a craving for a pre-war treat. The dish comes out of the oven with a crunchy crust.

550g (1lb 3oz) sausage meat	2 teaspoons chopped sage
225g (8oz) onions, peeled and grated	sugar to taste (optional)
	vegetable oil, for greasing
225g (8oz) cooking apples, peeled and grated	vegetable oil, for greasing

Preheat the oven to 180°C (350°F) gas mark 4.

Spread half the sausage meat into a well-greased baking tin or shallow casserole. Top with the onions, apples and sage. If the apples are very tart, sprinkle on some sugar.

Add the rest of the sausage meat and shape this top layer to look as much like a duck as possible.

Bake in the preheated oven for 45–50 minutes.

Adapted from *Feeding the Nation* by Marguerite Patten

MOCK FISH PIE
(ARTICHOKE GRATIN)

Serves 4

There is nothing remotely fishy about this dish, but it's an excellent artichoke gratin. Artichokes are unaccountably neglected. Easy to grow in the garden, they make delicious soup, can be roast alongside potatoes to eat with the Sunday joint or mashed half and half with potatoes.

450g (1lb) Jerusalem artichokes
1 teaspoon vinegar
115g (4oz) grated Cheddar cheese
55g (2oz) breadcrumbs
a pinch of cayenne pepper
salt and freshly ground black pepper

for the white sauce:
25g (1oz) butter
1 tablespoon plain flour
300ml (½ pt) milk

Preheat the oven to 180°C (350°F) gas mark 4.

Peel the artichokes and put them immediately in a bowl of cold water with the vinegar added to prevent them discolouring.

To make the sauce, melt the butter in a saucepan, stir in the flour and cook for a minute. Add the milk slowly, stirring all the time until the sauce thickens. Remove from the heat and set aside.

Cut the artichokes into pieces the size of a small oyster, put them into a saucepan of cold, salted water. Bring to the boil and simmer for about 10 minutes until just tender.

Mix together the cheese, breadcrumbs and cayenne pepper. Season with salt and pepper.

Put half the artichokes in a greased ovenproof dish, then a layer of half the breadcrumb mixture, then the rest of the artichokes. Pour the sauce over and spread the rest of the breadcrumb mixture on top.

Bake in the preheated oven for 15–20 minutes until golden brown.

From *Good Eating: Suggestions for Wartime Dishes* (*Daily Telegraph*)

FOOD FACTS

The Ministry of Food did their best to show people how to stretch their rations to make healthy and palatable meals, by advertising, broadcasting and distributing leaflets explaining Food Facts.

One of the best things the Ministry did was to enlist the now legendary Marguerite Patten. As a Home Economist employed in the electrical industry, she gave cooking demonstrations using luxury ingredients, which were to vanish soon after war was declared. She then switched to devising economical recipes for healthy family meals, travelling up and down the country with her colleagues, giving practical demonstrations in town halls, markets, department stores and factory canteens, often in the evenings, when working women could attend. They also visited hospitals and welfare centres to advise patients, pregnant women and mothers of babies. Marguerite also broadcast regularly on *The Kitchen Front*, and was later to become a much loved TV cook and writer of cookery books.

Certain foods were promoted as essential to good health, especially for children. Recipes for dishes using vegetables, the one unrationed food category of high nutritional value, were high on the agenda. Nowadays we're on to this again, with our five-a-day rule.

First and foremost, good old Potato Pete really knew his onions. The campaign to promote potatoes as a substitute for bread was a great success, and by the end of the war sixty per cent more potatoes were being eaten than at its start.

MIRACLE FOODS 1: ONE POTATO, TWO POTATO

'There was an old woman who
   lived in a shoe.
She had so many children she
   didn't know what to do.
She gave them potatoes instead
   of some bread,
And the children were happy
   and very well fed.'
   Ministry of Food advertisement

THE VERSATILE BAKED POTATO

Baked potatoes offer extra nutrition in their skins, and are one of the easiest meals to prepare: a quick scrub and they are ready for the oven. Here are some different ways to treat them:

CHEESE

cut a baked potato in half, scoop out the insides, mix with grated cheese, season and put back into the skins. Return to the oven until browned on top.

PIGS IN CLOVER

before baking, take out the centre of each potato with an apple corer. Fill the hole with a skinned sausage, then bake the potatoes. Serve with chopped, lightly cooked cabbage.

OTHER IDEAS FOR FILLINGS

left-over curry; leftover spicy mince; broccoli bits in crème fraîche; chopped cooked chicken with cream and fresh herbs; chopped chorizo; spicy prawns with mushrooms; a kidney wrapped in thin bacon; a boiled egg; scambled egg; bacon.

CHAMP

Serves 4

Delicious, but a profligate use of butter by wartime standards

675g (1lb 8oz) potatoes, peeled
250ml (½ pt) warm milk
6 spring onions, finely sliced

55g (2oz) butter
salt and freshly ground black pepper

Boil the potatoes, then drain them and add the milk. Mash until really smooth. Season to taste and stir in the spring onions. Put a mound of potato on each plate, make a well in the centre and put in a knob of butter. Eat immediately.

POTATO FLODDIES

Serves 4

This unusual recipe from Food Facts, published by the Ministry of Food is really a potato fritter. It works well as a savoury dish with, say, freshly made tomato sauce, or, if something more substantial is wanted, a fried egg on top. Served with jam and a blob of clotted cream or crème fraîche it makes a rather wicked pudding.

4 medium-sized potatoes
4 tablespoons plain flour
4 tablespoons chopped mixed herbs
  (optional)
dash of cayenne pepper (optional)

4 tablespoons of dripping or
  vegetable oil
salt and freshly ground black pepper

Peel the potatoes and grate them into a bowl. Add sufficient flour to form a stiff batter. Season with salt and pepper. If you want it as a savoury dish, add the chopped mixed herbs and cayenne pepper to the batter.

Heat a little dripping or oil until very hot in a frying pan. Drop heaped tablespoons of the mixture into it. When brown on one side, turn and brown on the other, about 4 minutes each side.

Serve with a little jam or lemon juice and sugar if you want to serve these as a sweet dish.

MIRACLE FOODS 2: BACK TO YOUR ROOTS

In January 1942 there was a carrot surplus of some 100,000 tons and, in order to help shift them, the Ministry of Food invented a colleague for Potato Pete. Doctor Carrot (the children's best friend) reinforced the myth that carrots help you see in the dark (see page 65).

Eating plenty of carrots was said to improve RAF pilots night vision. Sure enough, the success rate of British pilots, particularly the renowned 'Cats-eye' Cunningham, in shooting down enemy bombers, increased noticeably. Naturally every little boy (and a few gullible big boys) wanted to eat up his carrots. Actually, the secret of the pilots success was not so much carrots as the secret introduction of airborne radar. By putting it about that there was a secret ingredient in the pilots diet, the Government hoped to conceal the new technology from the Nazis. Whether the enemy believed the story or not, on the home front carrot consumption rapidly increased.

Recommended recipes at the time included Carrot Hotpot, Carrot Croquettes, Curried Carrots, Carrot Fudge, Carrolade (a drink combining carrot juice with the juice of Swedes) and Carrot Marmalade.

The Ministry of Food also made a series of filmed Food Flashes between ten and twenty seconds long, shown in cinemas. One showed Potato Pete with three carrots. The voice-over said, 'Whilst remembering the potato, don't forget our old friend, the carrot. They are ideal for night blindness – but not this kind, of course!' – cut to a final shot of a drunk staggering down the street and swinging on a lamp post.

There was nothing a carrot could not do, apparently, although one wartime child remembered how his father, after a single mouthful of carrot marmalade, simply picked up the pot, walked out and emptied it on the compost heap.

The other root vegetables – swedes, turnips, celeriac and parsnips – are excellent in soups and stews, or when cooked until soft and added to an equal quantity of boiled potatoes to make a mash with attitude. Grated parsnips mixed with cream and seasoned with plenty of black pepper make a delicious gratin with a crust of breadcrumbs. In wartime cream was out of the question, but a well-flavoured stock could have been successfully substituted. The result would be different but still tasty.

TURN OVER A NEW LEAF

Eat Vegetables daily
to enjoy good health

MOCK APRICOT FLAN

Serves 8

Judging by the colour and texture of the filling, you might think apricots were involved, but it doesn't taste of apricots. Nor does it taste of carrots or plum jam. The flavour is pleasant but elusive – definitely more fruity rather than vegetable. I give the recipe for Potato Pastry out of interest and because it is palatable, but a rich shortcrust pastry made with half flour, half ground almonds would result in a classier flan.

for the potato pastry:
175g (6oz) self-raising flour
pinch of salt
70g (2½oz) cooking fat or butter
55g (2oz) potato, peeled and grated
1–2 tablespoons ice-cold water

for the filling:
450g (1lb) young carrots, grated
4 tablespoons of water
4 tablespoon plum jam
¼ teaspoon almond essence

preheat the oven to 200°C (400°F) gas mark 6.

Sift the flour and salt into a large bowl. Rub the fat or butter into the flour, add the potato and mix. Add enough water to bind the dough.

Roll out on a floured surface and use it to line a 23cm (9in) flan case. Prick the base all over with a fork.

Bake in the preheated oven for 15 minutes until golden brown.

Meanwhile make the filling. Put the carrots in a saucepan along with the water, 2 tablespoons of the jam, and the almond essence.

Simmer gently until a soft pulp is formed. This may take as long as an hour.

Spread the mixture into the pastry case. Melt the rest of the jam with a tablespoon of water and use it to glaze the tart.

BEETROOT PUDDING

Serves 4

Carrots were not the only root for which the Ministry devised cunning new recipes. *The Ministry's Food Facts leaflet No. 40* had a recipe using the sweetness of beetroot to make 'a nice sweet pudding with very little sugar.' I cooked this out of curiosity. It was more like a cake than a pudding, with a nice crunchy top but the colour was a hideous murky pink. It lacked flavour but for this I blame the supermarket beetroot I used. A freshly dug, home-grown one would be sweeter and earthier. I have used butter rather than 'fat' in the original recipe, and more of it, added more sugar and an orange, which has an affinity with beetroot, for extra flavour.

butter, for greasing
175g (6oz) wholemeal flour
1 teaspoonful baking powder
55g (2 oz) butter
55g (2oz) sugar

115g (4oz) cooked or raw beetroot, very finely grated
juice and zest of 1 orange
150ml (5fl oz) milk

Set the oven at 180°C (350°F) gas mark 4. Grease a 18cm (7in) cake tin or pie dish.

Mix the flour with the baking powder. Rub together the butter, sugar and beetroot.

Mix in the orange juice and zest. Add enough milk to give the mixture a soft consistency.

Turn it into the tin or dish and bake for 35–40 minutes, or until a skewer pushed into the centre of the cake comes out clean.

Serve as a pudding with orange segments or as a cake for tea or elevenses.

CHOCOLATE AND BEETROOT BROWNIES

Makes about 20

I don't see all of the wartime ersatz recipes going down too well with the children (or the adults) in my family. But a large plateful of Chocolate and Beetroot Brownies disappeared in no time at all.

55g (2oz) good-quality dark chocolate (70% cocoa solids), broken into chunks
250g (9oz) unsalted butter, cut into cubes, plus more for greasing

3 eggs
250g (9oz) caster sugar
150g (5½oz) wholemeal self-raising flour
250g (9oz) beetroot, boiled until tender, peeled and grated

Preheat the oven to 180°C (350°F) gas mark 4. Grease a 20x30cm (9x12in) baking tin and line the bottom with baking paper.

Put the chocolate and butter in a heatproof bowl. As the oven begins to warm up, put the bowl on one of the shelves for a few minutes until the chocolate and butter start to melt. Stir, and put back into the oven for a few more minutes to melt completely.

Whisk the eggs and sugar together in a large bowl until combined, then beat in the melted chocolate and butter until smooth.

Gently fold in the flour then the beetroot – be careful not to over-mix or it will make the brownies tough.

Pour the mixture into the prepared tin and smooth the top with a spatula. Bake in the preheated oven for about 20 minutes. A knife or skewer pushed into the middle should come out with a few moist crumbs clinging to it.

Don't be tempted to overcook them! Remove the tin from the oven and leave on a wire rack to cool before cutting into squares.

From *River Cottage Every Day* by Hugh Fearnley-Whittingstall

NOT LORD WOOLTON'S PIE

Serves 6

It seems that nobody liked His Lordship's pie. The wartime recipe would have been much improved by the addition of an onion (probably unobtainable then), garlic, herbs and a well-flavoured stock. Here is a tasty modern version. The quantity of each vegetable is not important; just use what is available.

1kg (2lb 4oz) mixed winter vegetables, such as a carrot, a parsnip, half a celeriac, 2 small turnips, 2 Jerusalem artichokes and some swede.
2 tablespoons olive oil
1 large onion, peeled and thinly sliced
1 large garlic clove, finely chopped
300ml (½pt) chicken stock

3 tablespoons chopped fresh herbs, such as parsley, thyme, marjoram and a bay leaf
salt and freshly ground black pepper

for the topping:
900g (2lb) floury potatoes, peeled
55g (2oz) butter
about 200ml (7fl oz) milk
115g (4oz) Cheddar cheese, grated

Preheat the oven to 220°C (425°F) gas mark 7.

Cut the vegetables into uniform dice about 2½cm (1in).

Heat the olive oil in a wide, shallow saucepan and add the onion. Cook it gently until transparent. Add the garlic and cook for a minute more. Remove the onion and garlic to an ovenproof pie dish.

Turn up the heat a little, add more oil if necessary and turn the vegetables in the oil until they start to colour. Add enough stock to prevent them sticking to the pan, and stir occasionally, until the liquid has evaporated. At this stage the vegetables should still be slightly crunchy. Season and put them in the pie dish. Sprinkle with the herbs.

Meanwhile boil the potatoes for the topping. When the potatoes are cooked, mash them with the butter, milk, cheese and season with plenty of freshly ground black pepper.

Cover the pie with the mash, rough up the surface with a fork and cook in the oven until the top is brown, about 20 minutes.

Variations: As a topping, use pastry or overlapping thin slices of raw potato. Try adding a chopped apple to the vegetables and replace half the stock with cider.

eat

EAT greens
FOR HEALTH

Daily

No. 19,345

FEED RIGHT
TO FEEL RIGHT

MIRACLE FOODS 3: EAT UP YOUR GREENS

As a wartime child I dreaded the phrases 'drink up your milk' and 'eat up your greens'. My milk was tepid and came in a pewter christening mug that seemed to impart a metallic flavour to its contents. The greens were fibrous, over-cooked and often floating in a pool of water. I must be grateful, looking back, that nobody imposed on me the Oslo breakfast (or dinner or tea), consisting of wholemeal bread, milk, butter or margarine, cheese and raw greens. Nobody seemed to know what it had to do with Oslo, but the Radio Doctor reported that London children on this diet '...literally bloomed. From green cabbage leaves to red rosy cheeks.'

Dr Hill advocated salads of raw cabbage, broccoli, Brussels sprouts and young dandelion. Watercress and mustard and cress were also recommended, but lettuce and cucumber 'practically useless for vitamin C'. The Radio Doctor's sound dietary advice to eat something raw and green every day still holds good, and following it need not be a penance. Shredded raw cabbage leaves can be sweet and crunchy; try them garnished with croutons, crispy bacon bits or toasted nuts.

Interesting salads were never one of the strengths of British home cooking. Until quite recently a few limp lettuce leaves, half a tomato, a small heap of raw carrot and a sprinkling of cress was the norm. The dressing was either non-existent or came out of a bottle. But salad need never be boring; there are so many delicious permutations and combinations. You can also add variety by using different oils in the dressing: walnut oil, hazelnut oil and hemp seed oil each add their own distinctive taste, and can be sharpened with orange or lemon juice or raspberry vinegar instead of more traditional wine vinegar.

SOME GOOD SALAD COMBINATIONS

SPINACH, WATERCRESS, TOASTED PINE NUTS

WALDORF SALAD: WALNUTS, APPLES, CELERY, GRAPES, MAYONNAISE

RAW CARROT, CELERIAC AND CUCUMBER BATONS

SWEETHEART CABBAGE WITH TOASTED SESAME SEEDS, HONEY, GARLIC AND GINGER DRESSING

RED CABBAGE, NUTS, RAISINS

COOKED BEETROOT, GREEN BEANS TOMATOES

BRUSSELS SPROUTS, CELERY, TOASTED PUMPKIN SEEDS WITH OLIVE OIL AND BALSAMIC VINEGAR DRESSING

FLAPJACKS

Makes 12-16

Unlike wartime cooks, we now need no persuading to add oats to toppings for fruit crumbles, or to make flapjacks for a lunchbox or teatime snack.

55g (2oz) butter or margarine, plus extra for greasing	55g (2oz) Demerara sugar
115g (4oz) golden syrup	225g (8oz) rolled oats

Preheat the oven to 180°C (350°F) gas mark 4. Grease a 20cm (8in) square, shallow cake tin.

In a saucepan melt the butter, syrup and sugar. Stir in the oats and turn the mixture into the cake tin, spreading it evenly. Bake in the preheated oven for 30–35 minutes.

Take out of the oven and cut into square or rectangular pieces immediately, leaving it in the tin until completely cold before removing.

MIRACLE FOOD 4: OATMEAL

Oatmeal, according to the Ministry's Food Facts, gives you energy, protects you from illness and makes strong bones and healthy blood. In wartime it also had the virtue of being home-grown and, thanks to a Government subsidy, it cost less than 3½ d a pound. Housewives were urged to use oatmeal to bulk out other foods, mixing it with flour for cakes and pastry, thickening soups with it and adding it to savoury puddings and pies to make the precious meat ration go further. Oatmeal porridge for breakfast is still the best possible start to the day. Eat it standing up (wearing a kilt?) like a true Scot with nothing added except salt, or add milk and dribble on honey or golden syrup, or add a blob of jam.

MIRACLE FOOD 5: CHEESE

The Radio Doctor: 'A cheese of 20lb contains as much nutriment as a sheep's carcase of 60lb.'

During the Second World War the 2oz per person per week cheese ration didn't go far. Most of us can eat 2oz at a sitting, whether it's grated in a lunchbox sandwich, or cooked as a soufflé, or as a bubbling brown sauce on cauliflower cheese or macaroni cheese, or grilled on toast as Welsh rabbit. Today, fortunately there's no restriction on how much cheese we can buy, and it's a great source of protein.

Waverley Oats
Specially made to nourish Children
WAVERLEY OATS
For Perfect Porridge
1 LB. NET.
M.W.

RABBIT CASSEROLE

Serves 6

Of course, rabbit makes a delicious dish in its own right and there is no need for it to masquerade as chicken, but in the war years it lacked glamour. Today, perhaps because it is not available on every supermarket shelf, it seems quite adventurous to cook and eat rabbit. Its texture is even denser than that of chicken. If you are not sure of the age of the rabbit, or how far it has run, slow cooking in a casserole will ensure tender meat.

1 tablespoon plain flour
1 large rabbit, or 2 small, jointed
   into 6 pieces by the butcher
55g (2oz) butter
1 large onion, peeled and sliced
300ml (10½ fl oz) white wine
2 celery sticks, roughly chopped
2 medium carrots, roughly
   chopped
2 large garlic cloves, peeled and
   crushed

1 bunch of fresh thyme
1 bay leaf
1 litre (1¾pts) hot chicken stock
300ml (10½ fl oz) double cream
100g (3½ oz) mushrooms, thinly
   sliced
salt and freshly ground black
   pepper

Season the flour with salt and pepper, put it on a plate and lightly coat the rabbit pieces.

In a heavy-based pan melt half the butter and, in batches, turn the rabbit pieces until lightly browned all over. Transfer to a casserole and keep warm.

In the pan soften the onion, adding more butter if needed. Add the wine, bring to the boil and continue boiling briskly until the volume of liquid has reduced by half.

Tuck the celery, carrots, garlic, thyme and bay leaf around the rabbit pieces in the casserole, making everything fit snugly. Pour the wine and onion mixture over. Add enough hot stock to just cover the rabbit pieces.

Bring the mixture to the boil and simmer very, very gently, uncovered, for 1–1¼ hours, until the rabbit meat is tender and the sauce has thickened. Alternatively, you could cook it in an oven preheated to 120°C (250°F) gas mark ½, in which case, put a lid on the pot.

When cooked transfer the rabbit pieces to a warmed dish, cover and set aside to keep warm. Remove the vegetables to a separate bowl.

Bring the liquid in the casserole to the boil and boil hard until the sauce has reduced and thickened.

Lower the heat until the sauce is just simmering and stir in the cream. Simmer for about 10 minutes until the cream sauce has thickened slightly.

Taste, adjust the seasoning, then strain the sauce over the rabbit pieces. Simmer for 8–10 minutes, or until the rabbit has warmed through.

Meanwhile, melt the remaining butter in a small pan, add the chopped mushrooms and cook until soft. Add them to the rabbit and cream sauce and serve.

Tip: For a more elegant dish, take the rabbit meat off the bones after it is cooked and before you make the sauce.

MAKING THE MOST OF MEAT

Much of the Ministry's propaganda was aimed at persuading people to eat less meat and more eggs (albeit dried), milk and cheese. But it was hard to wean them away from the meat-and-two-veg tradition. In order to put meat on the table, women learned to use off-the-ration meat that they had never encountered before: chicken was not rationed but was practically unobtainable, so rabbit appeared regularly in its place. I remember seeing my mother's face flush with triumph when my father congratulated her on cooking a delicious chicken fricassee – actually it was rabbit.

Even my mother, intrepid and skilful cook that she was, drew the line at whale-meat. It became available from 1945, usually in fishmongers rather than butchers, and was universally unpopular. In a Falmouth hotel, the chef grilled it as if it were beef steak. One guest promptly sent it back – a brave thing to do with any dish in those days – and the other diners followed suit. Even the dog would not touch it.

Others who tried whale meat rejected it as 'horrible', 'repulsive', 'revolting', 'ghastly'. 'Like a lump of cod liver oil', or 'like fishy liver' were other descriptions. One cook went to great trouble to disguise it. 'It had been soaked overnight, steam-cooked, and soaked again, then blanketed with a sauce. But still it tasted exactly what it sounds like – tough meat with a distinctly fishy flavour, ugh. Just this once the next-doors cat ate it!'

The comment in Punch magazine was, '"Fry your whale-meat with an onion to absorb the oil," advises a chef, "and throw away the onion." As well?'

FAVOURITE CHEAP CUTS

BEEF:
brisket, skirt, oxtail, shin

LAMB OR MUTTON:
breast, middle neck, scrag end of neck

PORK:
belly, hock, spare ribs, trotter

As the meat ration was regulated by price not weight, cheaper cuts were excellent value – and still are. All benefit from long, slow cooking with gentle heat, and, because they tend to be quite fatty, can be cooked the day before they are eaten, so that when the dish has cooled, excess fat, which will have risen to the top, can be skimmed off.

A pot-roast, stew or casserole in which the vegetables are cooked with the meat, is also economical of fuel. The addition of herbs, garlic and wine or cider, which were used very sparingly if at all in wartime cooking, makes these dishes alluringly aromatic. The following three recipes, using cheap cuts of beef, lamb and pork, will do stalwart duty for good-value Sunday lunches.

STUFFED, ROLLED
BREAST OF LAMB

Serves 4

This recipe from the cottage smallholder's website (www.cottagesmallholder.com), for slow baked breast of lamb stuffed with chicken livers, apricots and pine nuts is a far cry from the wartime version in which the stuffing would have consisted mainly of breadcrumbs and/or oatmeal. The ingredients give it a Middle Eastern character.

500g (1lb 2oz) boned breast of lamb
3 small red onions, peeled and sliced
6 tablespoons cider

for the stuffing:
2 tablespoons olive oil
70g (2½ oz) onion, finely chopped
200g (7oz) chicken livers, very finely chopped

55g (2oz) dried apricots, very finely chopped
1 garlic clove, finely chopped
handful fresh coriander, very finely chopped
25g (1oz) pine nuts, toasted under the grill until golden brown
25g (1oz) sesame seeds, toasted under the grill until golden brown
100g (3½ oz) fresh breadcrumbs

Preheat the oven to 220°C (400°F) gas mark 6.

First make the stuffing. Heat the oil in a frying pan and gently fry the onion until it is soft and translucent.

Add the chicken livers, apricots, garlic, coriander, pine nuts and sesame seeds. Mix well. Spread the stuffing along the centre of the lamb. Roll up gently and secure with a butcher's skewer.

The stuffing will want to squeeze out, so place the meat in a boat of kitchen foil and cover the ends of the joint with two circles of foil to stop the stuffing burning. Lay the whole lot in a large roasting tin and put in the preheated oven for 30 minutes.

Spoon the red onions into the foil parcel beneath the meat and pour in half the cider. Reduce the heat to 160°C (325°F) gas mark 3 and return the joint to the oven for 2½ hours, basting occasionally.

Remove from the oven and allow the meat to rest for half an hour.

Tip away the fat in the roasting tin, reserving the juices from the joint. Add the remaining cider and simmer to thicken and reduce the sauce. Serve the lamb sliced with the red onions.

BOILED BEEF AND CARROTS (AND DUMPLINGS)

Serves 6

'Boiled beef and carrots,
Boiled beef and carrots,
That's the stuff for your Derby Kell,
Makes you fit and keeps you well.
Don't live like vegetarians
On food they give to parrots,
Blow out your kite, from Morn till night,
On boiled beef and carrots.'
Derby Kell is old Cockney rhyming slang for belly (Derby Kelly).

1.6kg (3lb 8oz) salted silverside or brisket of beef (ask the butcher to salt it)
3 onions, peeled
8 cloves
bouquet garni (sprigs of parsley, thyme and bay leaf tied together)
10 black peppercorns

2 small turnips, peeled and quartered
2 celery sticks, cut in 4cm (1½ in) lengths
2 leeks, trimmed, washed and cut into 5cm (2in) lengths
18 small carrots or larger carrots sliced lengthways

Soak the meat in cold water for several hours to get rid of the salt.

Put the beef in a large saucepan, add just enough water to cover and bring slowly to the boil. Skim the surface. Stick the onions with the cloves and add to the saucepan with the bouquet garni, peppercorns, turnips, celery and leeks. Lower the heat and simmer very gently for about 2 hours, or cook in an oven preheated to 150°C (300°F) gas mark 2.

Add the carrots and simmer gently for a further 30–40 minutes until the carrots are tender.

Transfer the beef and carrots to a warmed dish. Skim any fat from the surface of the cooking liquor, then strain it into a clean saucepan. Boil to reduce slightly, then pour it into a warm jug.

Carve the beef and serve with the carrots, the sauce and either mashed potatoes or Herby Dumplings (see page 160).

HERBY DUMPLINGS

Makes about 8

A good filler-up of stomachs and mopper-up of sauce, to eat with warming winter stews and casseroles.

175g (6oz) self-raising flour
85g (3oz) suet, grated
pinch of salt

2 tablespoons of chopped
parsley or mixed herbs

Mix everything in a bowl and add enough cold water to make a workable dough. Knead the dough until it is elastic and chill for 15 minutes.

Shape the dough into balls the size of walnuts. Cook on top of a simmering stew or in a pan of stock.

ROAST PORK BELLY

Serves 4

Pork belly is cheap because it's fatty, but don't let that put you off. As with all meat, it is the fat that imparts the flavour, and much of the fat disappears during cooking. The rest can be saved for frying. The scored skin makes wonderful crackling.

500–750g (1lb 2oz– 1lb 10oz)
 pork belly (ask the butcher to
 bone it and score the skin)
150g (5½ oz) fresh breadcrumbs
a bunch of sage leaves, chopped

1 onion, peeled and finely
 chopped
Worcestershire sauce, to taste
salt and freshly ground black pepper
kitchen string

Preheat the oven to 220°C (425°F) gas mark 7.

Rub plenty of salt into the gaps between the scored skin of the pork. This will help it to crisp in the oven.

Make the stuffing: mix together the breadcrumbs, sage, onion, and a couple of shakes of Worcestershire sauce. Season with pepper. Spread the stuffing on the inside of the belly.

Roll up the belly and tie securely with kitchen string. Place in a large roasting tin.

Roast in the preheated oven for 15–20 minutes, then reduce the oven temperature to 170°C (325°F) gas mark 3 and cook for a further 1½ hours.

If the crackling has not bubbled up and crisped, cut it away from the meat and put it under a hot grill for a few moments. Watch like a hawk to see it doesn't burn.

Serve sliced with pieces of the crackling on the side.

Cookery
Demonstrations

FOOD
IS A MUNITION OF WAR
DONT WASTE IT

OFFAL

Plenty of people are suspicious of tripe and other rarely encountered kinds of offal – we all tend to be wary of the unknown, especially when it comes to food, and you will not often find brains, hearts or sweetbreads (delicious in a restaurant but fiddly to prepare at home) in the butcher's shop. But liver and kidneys are readily available, and are, according to the Radio Doctor 'very solid organs stuffed full of food... If you've a tendency to gout, lay off liver and kidneys. If you haven't, they're the goods.' Being very solid organs, a little goes a long way, but they can be delicious. For Kidneys in Red Wine (see page xx). Calves liver, sliced thin and fried with bacon and onions, is quick, easy and hard to beat. The secret of success is not to overcook it; a minute each side is usually enough.

FEGATO ALLA VENEZIANA

Serves 4

This is the Venetian way of cooking liver. Almost every restaurant in Venice serves a slightly different version of this classic. Some leave out the sage, but it makes all the difference. Calves' liver is not always easy to come by but you can usually order it in advance from your friendly butcher. Nowadays he doesn't have to keep it under the counter for you.

olive oil
2 large onions, thinly sliced
about 15 sage leaves

500g (1lb 2oz) calves' liver,
    very thinly sliced and cut
into
    4cm (1½ in) squares
1 glass dry white wine

In a large frying pan heat 2 tablespoons of olive oil and cook the onion over a low heat until soft and beginning to brown. This will take about 20 minutes. Remove the onions with a slotted spoon and put aside to keep warm.

Put enough olive oil into a small saucepan to cover the bottom to a depth of 2½cm (1in). Heat the oil and fry the sage leaves, a few at a time, until crisp but not brown – they only take a few seconds. Drain on kitchen paper.

In the frying pan add one or two more tablespoons of oil and heat until it is almost smoking. Add the liver in one layer (if necessary cook it in two or more batches), and as soon as it is browned turn it over. It is important not to overcook it; the whole process only takes a few minutes.

Transfer the liver to a warmed dish with the onions and keep warm. Pour off any remaining oil from the pan then tip the wine into the pan. Stir well and simmer for 1–2 minutes, then pour over the liver and serve, garnished with the fried sage leaves.

SPAM FRITTERS

Serves 2

It would be wrong to leave the subject of meat in wartime without referring to those two great storecupboard standbys, corned beef and Spam, both off the ration and usually available on points. Corned Beef Hash and Spam Fritters are right up with Heinz baked beans on my list of comfort food. I've therefore included this recipe for old times sake. Those who are of an age to remember Spam divide into two camps. In one are those who hope never to have to taste it again. I am in the other camp – we are secretly addicted and the best way to eat Spam is as fritters with plenty of sauce sloshed over them.

1 x 200g (7oz) tin Spam, cut
   into 1cm (½in) slices
vegetable oil, for frying

for the batter:
60g (2¼oz) self-raising flour

pinch of salt
1 egg
either 1 tablespoon milk and
   1 tablespoon water, or 2
   tablespoons beer

Sieve the flour and salt into a bowl and make a well in the centre. Break the egg into the well and beat, adding the milk and water (or beer) a little at a time until it is a coating consistency. You may not need all the liquid.

Put the batter in the fridge for 20 minutes.

Dip the spam slices in the batter until coated all over.

Heat some oil in a frying pan. When it is smoking hot, reduce the heat a little and lower the fritters into the oil. Fry until golden brown, turning once. Serve with plenty of tomato ketchup or brown sauce.

Variations: The basic fritter batter can be used in so many ways, both savoury and sweet: corned beef, sweetcorn, parsnip, seafood, courgette, apple, apricot, banana, peach, pineapple, raspberry or strawberry.

LEFTOVERS

'Ships and more ships are wanted for war materials. Less space can be spared for food. That's why we must all think of food in terms of ship-savers. Today's scraps are tomorrows Savouries.'

Ministry of Food

'Waste not, want not' is still the mantra for those who remember rationing. Some of us smooth out parcel paper and put it in a kitchen drawer for future use. We untie knots instead of cutting them and save the string. The paper the butter comes wrapped in is kept in the fridge to grease a cake tin or pie dish. And we try to use up every last scrap of food.

We strip all the meat off a chicken carcass or from the bones of a Sunday roast. The bones go into the stock pot with onions, carrots, the trimmings from celery and leeks, and a big bunch of herbs. The meat is added to a risotto or a bean stew; or chopped finely with onions, herbs and mushrooms to make a pancake filling; or minced and shaped into rissoles and quickly browned in the frying pan.

Even when only a little is left, a canny cook will find a way to avoid waste. Leftover vegetables can be chopped and added to soups. A heel of cheese can be grated and put in the freezer for a future gratin, sauce or pasta dish. The end of a loaf of bread can be whizzed into crumbs to add to a fruit crumble or savoury stuffing. A spare egg yolk can be added to a baked custard, egg whites can be whisked into meringues (they keep really well in the freezer and don't need thawing), or folded into whipped cream to lighten it. Waste not, want not.

HERBY CHICKEN AND MUSHROOM PANCAKES

Makes at least 8 pancakes

Pancakes are not just for Shrove Tuesday. Sweet or savoury and endlessly versatile, they make a little go a long way and are a great way to use leftovers for a swift and economical mid-week supper.

for the pancake batter:
225g (8oz) plain flour
2 eggs
pinch of salt
600ml (1pt) milk
2 tablespoons of chopped fresh herbs,
    such as chives, parsley, and tarragon
butter or oil, for frying

for the filling:
55g (2oz) butter
1 large onion, finely chopped
450g (1lb) mushrooms, chopped
chopped, cooked chicken (quantity
    according to whatever is available)
150ml (5fl oz) crème fraîche
salt and pepper

Preheat the oven to 180°C (350°F) gas mark 4.

To make the batter, put the flour, eggs, salt and half the milk into a blender and whiz until smooth. Gradually add the rest of the milk until the mixture is the consistency of single cream (you may not need all the milk). Leave the mixture to rest for half an hour.

Stir the chopped herbs into the pancake mixture.

Heat a teaspoon of butter or oil in a frying pan and pour in just enough batter to coat the bottom of the pan, tipping the pan to distribute the batter evenly. When the surface looks dry, ease a palette knife under the pancake and flip it over to cook the other side. Repeat until you have used up all the batter. Stack the pancakes until you are ready to fill them.

To make the filling, gently melt three quarters of the butter in a saucepan, add the onion and cook until the onion is transparent. Do not let it brown. Add the mushrooms, season and cook with the lid on until soft. Stir in the crème fraîche and cooked chicken.

Spread some of the mixture on each pancake and roll it up. Put the rolled pancakes in an ovenproof dish. Melt the remaining butter and dribble it over the pancakes. Bake in the preheated oven until heated through – about 20 minutes.

Tip: Try some of these alternative fillings – ham and cheese, chopped or minced chicken with cream and herbs, leeks in cheese sauce, salmon and dill, minced beef and chilli, or spicy prawns.

SHEPHERD'S PIE

Serves 4

It is worth getting a bigger Sunday joint than your family can eat at a sitting, in order to have some meat leftover for this perennial favourite. Shepherd's Pie is made with leftover cooked lamb or mutton; if made with beef it is Cottage Pie.

450–675g (1–1½ lb) potatoes
500g (1lb 2oz) cooked lamb
   (leftovers from the Sunday joint)
1 onion, finely chopped
1 large carrot, finely chopped, or
   leftover cooked carrots
oil or dripping, for frying

1 heaped tablespoon flour
300ml (10½ fl oz) stock
1 tablespoon Worcestershire sauce
55g (2oz) Cheddar cheese, grated
   (optional)
salt and freshly ground black
   pepper

Preheat the oven to 180°C (350°F) gas mark 4.

Boil the potatoes for 15 minutes in a large pan of salted water. Drain, mash and set aside.

Meanwhile, put the oil or dripping in a large frying pan and cook the onion and carrot gently until soft but not coloured. Remove from the pan with a slotted spoon and set aside.

Increase the heat, add more oil if necessary and brown the mince, stirring and turning it all the time. Return the onion and carrot to the pan and mix with the meat. Sprinkle the flour over and stir to brown the flour.

Add the stock and Worcestershire sauce and stir over the heat until thickened and smooth – you may not need all the stock, you don't want the mixture too sloppy.

Transfer the mixture to a pie dish. Cover with mashed potato. Use a fork to make furrows in the potato.

Bake in the preheated oven for 30 minutes, then sprinkle with grated cheese and bake for a further 10 minutes or brown under the grill.

LAMB CURRY

Serves 4

Another way to use any leftover meat (not just lamb) and vegetables. This dish is only very distantly related to a proper Indian curry, but not to be despised.

500g (1lb 2oz) cooked lamb
oil or dripping, for frying
1 onion, peeled and sliced
1 large carrot, sliced
4–6 teaspoons curry powder
  or paste, according to taste
1 heaped tablespoon plain flour

300ml (10½fl oz) stock
any leftover cooked vegetables,
  diced
200g (7oz) basmati rice
mango chutney and lime pickle,
  to serve

Cut the meat into bite-sized pieces.

In a saucepan, soften the onion and carrot in the oil or dripping. Add the curry powder or paste – the quantity depends on how hot you like your curry. Cook for a minute or two, stirring, to release the flavours.

Stir in the flour, then the stock, stirring all the time, and cook for a few minutes till the sauce is thickened and smooth.

Stir in the meat and cooked vegetables and simmer while the rice is cooking.

Put the rice in a large saucepan, cover with water, stir and bring to the boil. Simmer for 10–12 minutes until the rice is tender. Drain and serve with the curry along with some mango chutney and lime pickle.

PLANNING AHEAD

Careful planning has always been the key to economical use of scarce resources. During the war thrifty housewives made the most of precious fuel as well as the family's food rations. They followed the Ministry's advice, not to heat the oven for just one item but to fill it up, following the pre-war tradition of a baking day when enough cakes, biscuits and pies were prepared to last a week. With modern aids such as food processors and blenders, fridges and freezers, we can cram a baking day into just a few hours, and reduce our electricity or gas bill by filling the oven each time we use it. We can also use one hot plate instead of three by cooking vegetables, fish or chicken in foil parcels, stacked above each other in a steamer. It's not difficult to get into the habit of making double quantities of soups and stews, or fruit pies and crumbles and putting one into the freezer for another day.

Shopping and cooking are easier and more economical if you plan meals for several days at a time, or even on a weekly basis. Opposite are two example menus early in the war, one in Germany and one in Britain.

In Britain, country families who took evacuees were paid 8s 6d a week for each child. A report in the *Times* in October 1939 described how a Scottish woman fed five boys aged from six to twelve. She said they had gained weight and enjoyed their food. To judge from the amount of meat they ate, Scotland was suffering less deprivation than Germany at this stage in the war.

BRITAIN 1939

There were three meals a day (breakfast, dinner, and high tea) with vegetables and apples from the garden, and hot milk before an 8 o'clock bedtime. Breakfast: porridge and scrambled eggs, alternate days

SUNDAY

DINNER – Roast shoulder of lamb or mutton, cabbage, potatoes. Baked apple dumplings.

MONDAY

DINNER – Cold meat, potatoes and sprouts. Hot apple and custard.

TUESDAY

DINNER – Shepherd's pie, carrots and turnips. Currant dumplings, sugar.

WEDNESDAY

DINNER – Scotch broth, made with 3lb beef flank, barley, split peas, carrot, turnip and onion. Meat with potatoes.

THURSDAY

DINNER – Beef stew with vegetables and potatoes. Rice pudding.

FRIDAY

DINNER – Minced beef with onions. Tinned pineapple and custard.

SATURDAY

DINNER – Use up rest of mince. Baked bread pudding.

GERMANY 1939

The following menu is recommended to the German housewife on the German radio for the next three days:

TUESDAY

BREAKFAST – Soup made of rye flour, with bread.

LUNCH – Spinach soup, pumpkin, potatoes, and bacon.

SUPPER – Vegetable noodles and tea made from blackberries.

WEDNESDAY

BREAKFAST – Coffee, with milk, bread and jam.

LUNCH – Goulash made with venison and potato balls.

SUPPER – Vegetable and bread soup then flummery and berries.

THURSDAY

BREAKFAST – Flour soup and bread.

LUNCH – Vegetable soup, yeast puff pastry, and stewed fruit.

SUPPER – Bread, with various spreadings, such as remainders of venison, goulash, and synthetic butter mixed with herbs.

Celebrations

War or no war, Christmas came round every year, as did family birthdays. Couples still got married. Even if there was nothing special to celebrate, there might be the occasional knees-up in the village hall or at the local Army or Air Force base. The first party I ever went to was at RAF Rudloe Manor, near Corsham in Wiltshire. It was near my grandparents' house, and when the RAF played host to local children at Christmas my cousins and I were invited. I remember jellies in traffic light colours, triangular white bread sandwiches, and crackers with paper hats. After tea we played oranges and lemons and elbowed each other out of the way to have a go on a huge slide imported for the occasion. Most exciting of all, Father Christmas appeared with a sack of toys, having parked his sleigh outside.

There were many constraints on celebrations involving food and drink, but they were overcome with great ingenuity. People saved up their rations for special occasions, and forgot the war for a few hours, immersed in the fun of making cakes, sweets and treats. Icing sugar was unobtainable, but cakes could be iced with a mixture of dried milk, sugar and water, with cocoa powder added if chocolate icing was wanted. Wedding cakes were 'iced' with decorated cardboard. As raisins and sultanas were in short supply, gravy browning was often added to fruit cakes to disguise the paucity of fruit.

JELLIES MADE WITH FRESH FRUIT JUICE

Serves 6

A party wasn't a party without jellies, and, today they are still definitely celebratory with their translucent jewel colours. When made with fresh fruit they are also a healthy option. Use berries, as below, or take advantage of today's abundance of citrus fruit and squeeze oranges, lemons or limes. You could even cheat by using cartons of your favourite juices.

Choose from the following berries, or make your own cocktail by mixing two or more kinds: strawberries, raspberries, red currants, white currants, blackcurrants, blueberries, cranberries, mulberries, or loganberries

900g (2lb) berries
juice of half a lemon, strained, or 2
    tablespoons elderflower cordial
115g (4oz) granulated sugar (the
    natural sweetness of fruit varies
    so you may not need it all)

I sachet granulated gelatine to set
I pint juice or equivalent sheet
gelatin

Put the berries in a saucepan with just enough water to stop them sticking to the bottom. Cook over a gentle heat until the juices run, about 10 minutes.

Sieve the fruit into a bowl, squashing it down a bit to extract the juice then strain the juice through muslin.

Add the lemon juice or elderflower cordial (it brings out the flavour of the berries) and stir in sugar to sweeten the juice, tasting and adding until it tastes right. Make sure the sugar is completely dissolved. If the mixture tastes too strong, add some water.

Measure the sweetened juice. Add the gelatine, following the instructions on the pack. Pour into glasses or moulds and leave to set in the fridge, preferably overnight.

Serve in glasses or dip the moulds up to the rim in hot water and turn the jellies out.

ROSE HIP JELLY

Serves 6

Pure nostalgia for wartime children who remember the daily spoonful of rose-hip syrup, full of vitamin C. Gathering rosehips in the hedgerows is a very satisfying occupation. An old-fashioned walking stick with a hooked handle is useful to pull the branches down within reach.

500g (1lb 2oz) ripe rose hips, stripped from stems and washed
2 tablespoons lemon juice
1kg (2lb 4oz) crab or cooking apples, roughly chopped, including cores, pips and skin

about 225g (8oz) sugar
1 or 2 sachets of granulated gelatine or the equivalent of sheet gelatine. You will know the exact quantity when you measure the juice – see below

Put the hips into a large saucepan with the lemon juice and enough water to just cover. Bring to the boil and simmer until soft. This could take an hour or more; it depends how ripe they are.

Put the apples in a separate pan with just enough water to cover the bottom and cook until they are soft – this will take about 20 minutes. Add the apples to the hips and mash to extract as much juice as possible. Strain through muslin, preferably overnight.

Dissolve the sugar in the juice a little at a time until it tastes right. Measure the juice and add the gelatine according to the packet instructions.

Pour into glasses or moulds and leave to set in the fridge, preferably overnight.

Serve in glasses or dip the moulds up to the rim in hot water and turn the jellies out.

BIRTHDAYS

Ernest van Someren, a research chemist living in Hertfordshire, recorded several of his little daughter Laurie's birthdays. In January 1941, 'At about four, five children came with two mothers... They began with jellies and Kay had made a cake and iced it (real icing sugar bought by our daily help) and there were three candles. Laurie ate hard and took little notice of the visitors. After tea we played in the sitting room, blowing bubbles, knocking balloons about, blind man's buff, and a bit of hide the thimble, the party was a screaming success. It broke up soon after six...'

The following year the party had increased to nine children and four parents. As ice cream, when it could be obtained was scarcely palatable, being made with wholemeal flour, Kay van Someren hit on the idea of making imitation ices with stiff custard between wafers – a great success.

There were grown-up birthdays too. When Nella Last's son Arthur was 27 in August 1940, he asked for orange jelly and Viennese bread for his tea. Oranges being hard to come by and costing 4d each, she used a Rowntree's orange jelly, whipped when cold but not set, plus 3 beaten egg whites. The egg whites came courtesy of the hens she kept in the garden.

THE OK CORRAL
BIRTHDAY CAKE

Serves 8–10

cake ingredients as for Princess
  Birthday Cake (right)

for the icing and decoration:
115g (4oz) butter
285g (10oz) icing sugar

2 tablespoons cocoa powder
  mixed to a paste with a little
water
1 packet malted milk biscuits
2 packets chocolate finger biscuits
demerara sugar
toy cowboys and horses and,
  if possible, a wagon

Make the basic cake in the same way as for the Princess Birthday Cake (see right) and bake in a 9in square tin (for a big party make two cakes and ice them together to make a big rectangle). When the cake is cold, put it on a large tray or board lined with brown paper.

Beat the butter, icing sugar and cocoa together and smooth it over the top and sides of the cake, keeping back a little icing to use as glue. On one side of the cake use the malted milk biscuits vertically to form the walls and roof of an open-sided stable, sticking them together with icing. Use the chocolate fingers to make a fence around the edge of the cake. Sprinkle the Demerara sugar around the stable to make a sandy surface. Set up the toy cowboys for a shoot out.

PRINCESS BIRTHDAY CAKE

Serves 8–10

A cake like this appeared on my 8th birthday and I've never forgotten it. Eggs, butter and sugar were still rationed, so my mother must have saved them up for weeks. The lady's body was porcelain, not plastic, but her figure was much the same as Barbie's.

365g (12oz) butter, softened
365g (12oz) caster sugar
8 medium eggs
285g (10oz) plain flour
85g (3oz) self-raising flour
2–3 tablespoons milk

for the icing and decoration:
115g (4oz) butter
285g (10oz) icing sugar
sugar daisies and silver ball
  decorations
a Barbie doll wearing a strapless
  bandeau top

Preheat the oven to 160°C (325°F) gas mark 3. Grease a 1.1 litre (2pt) ovenproof pudding bowl.

With an electric whisk, beat the butter and sugar together until light and fluffy.

Add the eggs one at a time then fold in the sifted flour. The mixture should drop easily from a spoon. If it is too stiff, stir in some milk. Put the mixture into the pudding bowl and bake for about 1 hour. It is ready when a skewer pushed into the centre comes out clean.

If necessary, trim the top to make it level, loosen the sides with a flexible palette knife and turn the cake out onto a large plate or board. The cake is the Princess's crinoline skirt.

Make the icing by mixing together the butter and icing sugar. Spread the icing over the cake, keeping a tablespoonful back.

Decorate the skirt with swags of silver balls and flowers around the hem and at the loops of the swags. Remove Barbie's legs and press her waist into the centre of the cake and use the remaining icing to taper the skirt into her body. Make her a crown with kitchen foil.

Let's speed the things we make (for Hitler's birthday cake!)

PARTIES

Joan Charles, a Civil Servant working at the Ministry of Agriculture, exchanged letters with her fiancé, Tony Ross, an RAF officer stationed in North Africa. Their correspondence was donated to the Imperial War Museum. In a letter dated 23rd November 1943 Joan wrote:

'Dear Tony,
...Some friends took me to a party in the evening. The Army and ATS Officers at The Bedford were our hosts and hostesses. It was a lovely party – I wish you might have shared it. There was dancing, and so much chatter and laughter. There were two high spots in the evening – a young American found it impossible to resist jitterbugging even on such a tiny crowded floor. The General, very fat and generously red-tabbed, whether in hospitality or sheer delight no-one could say, attempted to jitterbug too! Then the food took my breath away! I thought for an instant I had been whisked away back to 1939. It was a feast from dainty sandwiches to chocolate layer cake beautifully iced and decorated. The secret lies with the ex-Café Royal cook of "B" Mess. Friday – the Ministry dance. We returned the Army's hospitality with tea and a stale bun!'

The Café Royal in London's Regent Street, where the cook of B Mess learned his trade, was the scene of an outing for 25-year-old Peter Baxter, a Cambridge graduate and RAF corporal. He, his wife, and brother- and sister-in-law met up for a day out in London and went to the Café Royal for lunch. Peter didn't comment on the food, but was scathing about some of the clientele. 'Vile place – it made me seethe with anger. We went into the lounge first to have a glass of beer before lunch. It was crowded with people of the kind I detest. The men, mostly officers, were not too bad, but the women... Ugh, they made me want to crawl up the wall! They sat there, perched on stools or reclining elegantly in chairs, holding cigarettes in painted fingers, talking in loud strident voices with clipped, affected county accents as they sipped their gin and cocktails.... What work do these painted parasites do to help the country? Is keeping officers amused a sufficient contribution to the war effort?'

TRADITIONAL PARTY SANDWICH FILLINGS

The best sandwiches for parties or buffets are made with the bread sliced thin, crusts cut off and each sandwich quartered into triangles. For some children, brought up on healthy wholemeal bread, white bread is as big a treat today as it was during the war.

JAM:
Just spread it on. Raspberry is most popular.

EGG AND CRESS:
Mash hard-boiled eggs with mayonnaise, season and sprinkle cress on top.

SARDINE:
Drain the oil from a tin of sardines, mash the sardines with a little mayonnaise, a squeeze of lemon and some black pepper.

CRAB:
Mash tinned or dressed crab with mayonnaise. Add a little cayenne pepper.

MARMITE AND CUCUMBER:
Spread Marmite thinly on the bread. Peel the cucumber and slice thinly.

TOMATO:
These should be slightly soggy. Peel the tomatoes and slice thinly. Season with salt and black pepper.

DEVILLED EGGS

Makes 24

These are good for picnics as well as parties. The filling can play host to a wealth of variations – try mashed anchovies or sardines and Worcestershire sauce; grated cheese and chives; or even mustard and chutney. There are endless possibilities.

12 small eggs
3 tablespoonfuls mayonnaise
3 teaspoons curry powder

a few thinly sliced pimentos,
anchovies and/or gherkins,
to garnish

Boil the eggs for 9 minutes. Plunge into cold water.

Remove the shells, cut the eggs in half lengthways and put the yolks in a bowl. Mash the yolks with a fork and beat in the mayonnaise and curry powder to taste.

Spoon the yolk mixture back into the egg halves. Garnish with strips of pimento, anchovy or gherkin, as preferred.

SAUSAGE ROLLS

Makes about 20

Good as blotting paper for alcohol at grown-up parties, as fillers-up of small tummies at children's celebrations, and as portable snacks for journeys and picnics, sausage rolls are best served hot, or at least warm.

1 x 500g (1lb 2oz) packet of flaky or puff pastry	500g (1lb 2oz) chipolata sausages 1 egg, beaten

Preheat the oven to 220°C (425°F) gas mark 7. Line a baking tray with parchment.

Take the chipolatas out of their skins.

Divide the pastry into three equal pieces and, on a floured surface, roll out one piece into a long rectangle, 10cm (4in) wide.

Arrange one third of the sausage meat in a continuous roll, making one long sausage, the length of the pastry.

Brush one long edge of the pastry with the beaten egg, fold the pastry over the sausage and seal the join. Cut into individual rolls, each about 5cm (2in) long.

Do the same with the other two pieces of pastry. Put the rolls on the baking tray and bake at the top of the preheated oven for 20–25 minutes. Check after 15 minutes and cover with foil if they are getting too brown. Serve hot or warm.

WEDDINGS

Eileen Potter, an evacuation officer for London County Council, described her sister's wedding at Brompton Oratory. The bride wore a pale grey costume and hat and wine-coloured georgette blouse. The Reception was at the Rembrandt Hotel, a stone's throw from the church. Fifteen guests sat at a round table enjoying 'plenty of wine and a good spread including Peach Melba made with fresh peaches, but no cake because of sugar rationing.'

In 1941 at Joan Dommett's wedding in East Devon 'plenty of wine' was out of the question, though for the toast there was a glass of wine, or port or sherry. 'There just wasn't the sort of drinking there is now,' Joan wrote in Colyton at War. 'Mum and I and my sisters prepared the food for the reception at my uncle's farm. 40 guests. Sandwiches, sausage rolls, bread and cheese, jellies and trifles and fruit salad. Quite

a spread it was. It took us several hours to put it together. The cake had to be iced chocolate, not white. There wasn't enough icing sugar for the baker to give us two tiers with royal icing. But enough to make white piping over the chocolate icing. It was delicious anyway and it looked good'.

A year later, Maggie Joy Blunt was allowed Saturday morning off to go to her cousin's wedding. The bride wore white and her bridesmaids were in dark green velvet carrying daffodils. The reception was at a hotel in Acton, and Maggie Joy was impressed by the food, provided at just four days' notice: chicken and ham sandwiches, trifle, fruit salad and cakes in quantity. She was less impressed by the drinks. When asked by a colleague on Monday morning if she had got tight at the wedding, she replied that it would have been impossible.

SUMMER FRUIT SALAD

Serves 8–10

The tinned fruit salad in thick, sweet syrup that was considered such a treat during the war would not pass muster now that we can go to the local Pick-Your-Own for fresh, seasonal fruit, and indulge ourselves at the greengrocer with imported fresh pineapples, melons and mangoes. For a summer party, a glass bowl of carefully chosen and garnished fruits is as refreshing to the eye as it is to the palate.

1kg (2lb 4oz) mixed fresh fruit including 3 or more of the following: melon, pineapple, green seedless grapes, strawberries, blueberries, cherries, peaches, bananas, or apples

2 tablespoons kirsch, elderflower cordial or infusion of vervaine (lemon verbena) leaves

for the syrup:
200g (7oz) sugar
150ml (5fl oz) water
juice of 1 lemon
a few mint leaves or sprigs of borage to garnish

In a saucepan add the sugar to the water and lemon juice and stir until dissolved. Boil briskly for 5 minutes. Leave to cool.

Cut up the melon and pineapple, peel the grapes, slice the strawberries. Lastly, so they don't turn brown, slice the bananas and peaches, peel and slice the apples.

Mix the fruit together, add the kirsch, elderflower or vervaine to the syrup and pour it over, using just enough to cover the fruit.

Variations: Use only red and black fruits: raspberries, red currants, blackcurrants and blueberries. Alternatively, try peaches or nectarines with raspberries.

CHRISTMAS

During the war chicken was hard to get hold of and expensive, so was something of a Christmas treat, turkey being an even greater rarity. Nella Last flavoured her chicken with sage and onion stuffing with added sausage meat as well as sausages cooked with the potatoes in a tin, sprouts and creamed celery.

Muriel Green, on leave from the Land Army, described her family's celebration succinctly: 'Xmas dinner of chicken (old hen) and wartime plum pudding and mince pies.' George Springett was equally laconic. 'As Mrs Robinson was unable to get a turkey, and some chickens which Alf promised to send didn't arrive, we had half a shoulder of mutton. The Robinsons were very disappointed but I didn't care.'

Christmas menus, as one might expect, were all fairly similar. A few dined on goose or duck instead of chicken. Many ate trifle as well as Christmas pudding and mince pies. Alcoholic drinks were hard to come by, except for an occasional bottle of port or Madeira won in a raffle. People made do with beer or cider. Nuts, figs and dates, fresh fruit, Stilton and gorgonzola were notably absent from most tables.

For David Hurford in Devon, Christmas was not very different from one in peacetime, except there were more children in the house – '11 including our evacuees. Our Christmases together were always special. Food was never short for people in the countryside. When we killed a pig we would share it with the next farm. My brother and I would haul the half-carcase across the fields and would be given such a welcome it would even include chocolate. Come December there were the turkeys to pluck, and then the great day itself would arrive… While people in the cities made do with whatever they could get, we had a feast. Mrs Crouch was a former chef, and her puddings and pies were to be marvelled at.'

Dried fruits were much sought-after at Christmas, for the pudding, the mince pies and the cake. Tony Ross included sultanas in one of the parcels he sent from North Africa, and Joan was duly grateful for this contribution towards the Christmas cake. 'It is dear of you to send these supplementary rations and we are glad of them,' she wrote. 'I am puzzled though at the cost, Tony — is it that the shopkeepers recognise you as inexperienced in household shopping! Or is the cost-of-living so high? Sultanas are 8p a pound in England, dear.'

MINCE PIES

Makes about 12

Christmas wouldn't be Christmas without mince pies in war time or peace time. The use of ground almonds in the pastry makes it very light and crumbly. The fat-free wartime recipe for Plum and Russet Mincemeat on page 189 is better than any kind bought in a jar, and doesn't need lemon juice added, although a little extra brandy or sloe gin is always welcome.

for the pastry:
85g (3oz) ground almonds
85g (3oz) plain flour
grated zest of 1 unwaxed lemon
85g (3oz) butter
1–2 tablespoons water

for the filling:
juice of 1 lemon
2 tablespoons rum or brandy
450g (1lb) jar of mincemeat
icing sugar, to dust

Preheat the oven to 200°C (400°F) gas mark 6. Grease a 12-hole tart tray.

Put all the pastry ingredients in a food processor and whiz until they are the texture of breadcrumbs.

Add the cold water a little at a time and pulse until the mixture forms a lump of dough. Rest it in the fridge for half an hour.

Stir the lemon juice and rum or brandy into the mincemeat.

Roll out the pastry on a well-floured surface, flouring the rolling pin frequently. Using a cutter, cut two discs for each pie, one larger than the other. Use the larger discs to line the tart tray.

Put a spoonful of mincemeat in each pie. Put the smaller pastry disc on top. Pinch the two discs together and use the tip of a knife to make a small hole in the top. Bake in the preheated oven for 20 minutes until golden brown.

WINTER FRUIT SALAD

Serves 8

Good as an antidote to rich Christmas food this can be made two or three days in advance, which has the added benefit of allowing the flavours to blend and mature.

1 quantity of syrup (see Summer
Fruit Salad, page 182)
250g (9oz) vacuum packed
   cooked chestnuts
250g (9oz) ready-to-eat dried
   apricots

1 vanilla pod, split lengthways
3 large oranges
2 tablespoons Cointreau or
   Grand Marnier

Put the chestnuts, apricots and vanilla pod in a saucepan and pour over enough syrup to just cover them. If there is not enough syrup, add water. Bring to the boil, simmer gently for 5 minutes and leave in the pan to cool.

With a sharp knife peel the oranges removing all the pith. Cut each segment away from its membrane, turning the membranes like the leaves of a book. Squeeze the skin and membranes to extract any remaining juice.

Gently stir the oranges and juice into the chestnut and apricot mixture, turn into a glass serving bowl and dribble the liqueur over. Chill until ready to serve.

BRANDY SNAPS

Make about 16

This Christmas favourite remains as popular today as during the Second World War. If you fancy a twist on the traditional filling of brandy cream, serve the snaps with gooseberry or rhubarb fool instead.

115g (4oz) butter
115g (4oz) caster sugar
115g (4oz) golden syrup
115g (4oz) plain flour
1 teaspoon ground ginger
juice of ½ lemon

for the filling:
300ml (10fl oz) double cream
2 tablespoons brandy

Preheat the oven to 180°C (350°F) gas mark 4. Line two baking sheets with baking parchment.

Melt the butter, sugar and syrup together in a pan. Add the flour, ginger and lemon and mix everything together thoroughly.

Drop teaspoonfuls of the mixture onto the baking sheets 15cm (6in) apart (they will spread while cooking). Bake in the preheated oven until golden brown.

While still warm and pliant, roll each one round the handle of a wooden spoon and slip it off.

Whip the cream with the brandy until stiff. Pipe the whipped cream into the snaps just before you serve them.

PLUM AND RUSSET MINCEMEAT

Makes 4 x 450g (1 lb) jars

This wartime recipe was sent in to *The Farmers' Weekly* by Miss Williams, Durham Field Farm, Shotley Bridge, Durham. Orchard fruit is used as a replacement for suet. The combination of fresh and dried fruit makes a light and fruity mixture which still retains the rich, warm spiciness of a traditional Christmas mincemeat. Pam Corbin who gave me this delicious recipe says 'It always works v. well and I ring the changes by using quince, apples or pear for the purée.'

1kg plums (1lb 2oz)
finely grated zest and juice of 2-3
    oranges (you need 200ml juice)
500g (1lb) russet apples, peeled,
    cored and chopped into 1cm cubes
200g (7oz) currants
200g (7oz) raisins
200g (7oz) sultanas
100g (3 ½ oz) orange marmalade

250g (9oz) Demerara sugar
½ teaspoon ground cloves
2 teaspoons ground ginger
½ nutmeg, grated
50ml (2fl oz) ginger wine or cordial
    (optional)
100g (3 ½ oz) chopped walnuts
50ml (2fl oz) brandy or sloe gin

Preheat the oven to 130°C (250°F) gas mark ½.

Wash the plums, halve and remove the stones, then put into a saucepan with the orange juice. Cook gently until tender, about 15 minutes. Blend to a purée in a liquidiser or push through a sieve. You should end up with about 700ml (1³/₄pt) plum purée.

Put the purée into a large bowl and add all the other ingredients, except the brandy or gin. Mix thoroughly, then cover and leave to stand for 12 hours.

Put the mincemeat in a large baking dish and bake, uncovered, for 2–2 ½ hours. Stir in the brandy or gin, then spoon into warm, sterilised jars, making sure there aren't any air pockets. Seal with a sterilised twist-on lid or a waxed paper disc and cellophane cover. Store in a dry, dark, cool place until Christmas. Use within 12 months.

NO TRIFLING MATTER

Trifle, which today seldom appears on any menu, at home or in a restaurant, was so much part of every wartime celebration that it deserves a special mention. It made an appearance at weddings, Christmas meals and other parties, and was everybody's pudding of choice.

Most Mondays, Pam Ashford would go to lunch at the Glasgow Soroptimist Club, where the meals were lavish. 'Marvellous lunch... broth, a big piece of fresh salmon, cucumber, lettuce, hard-boiled eggs, peas, followed by high helpings of trifle'. Trifle 'like a pre-war dream' appeared fairly regularly at the Soroptimists' lunches, sometimes left over from weddings at the weekends. 'Odd as it may sound,' Pam wrote, 'Captain Devlin who lives in London hotels was almost in tears over trifles there. They give him trifle day after day until he nearly screams when he sees the plate approaching him.'

I'm with the Captain on this. Compared to what a trifle can be, most wartime versions were sorry affairs made from stale cake, jelly cubes unacquainted with fruit, custard made from powder, and mock cream. There were some bizarre variations on this theme. The *Daily Telegraph's* book of readers' wartime recipes, *Good Eating*, gives a recipe for Cornish Trifle made from semolina, cocoa and marmalade. At my school (served without the cream) it was considered a treat, but not by me.

TRIFLE

Serves 8

My mother made the real thing, and it was excellent. I don't know where she got the cream in those days.

½ a sponge cake or 6 trifle sponges
raspberry or strawberry jam
150ml (5fl oz) sweet sherry or
   Marsala
450g (1lb) raspberries or
   strawberries, sliced
300ml (10½ fl oz) double cream
flaked almonds, toasted

for the custard:
4 egg yolks
1 tablespoon caster sugar
300ml (10½ fl oz) milk
300ml (10½ fl oz) single cream
1 teaspoon vanilla extract

Break up the sponge cake, spread jam on the pieces and put them at the bottom of a glass bowl. Sprinkle the sherry or Marsala over the cake.

When it has soaked in, scatter the strawberries or raspberries over the cake.

Make the custard: in a bowl, beat the egg yolks and sugar. In a saucepan, heat the milk and single cream together to boiling point and pour it slowly on to the egg yolks, stirring constantly. Put the mixture in a double boiler or a thick-bottomed saucepan and cook over a very low heat, stirring all the time.

When the custard thickens to the consistency of double cream, remove it from the heat and pour it straight into a cold bowl to reduce the heat.

When it is cold, pour it over the fruit.

Whip the double cream and spread it over the custard. Chill and, shortly before serving, scatter the almonds over the top.

Too good to waste!

BIRD'S
CUSTARD

★ Little people like big plates of BIRD'S CUSTARD. And from early days it is good for them . . . for BIRD'S is light, satisfying, easily digested.

BIRD'S CUSTARD AND JELLIES

AND FINALLY

On VE day the end of the war in Europe was celebrated in almost every street in almost every town. Children had the day off school, streets were closed to traffic and decorated with red white and blue bunting. Tables spread with table cloths and decorated with flowers were set up in the middle of the road. Every family contributed, overcoming rationing to cover the tables with an amazing array of food: sandwiches, cakes, jellies and blancmanges. There was singing and dancing and games and general rejoicing.

The period of post-war austerity gradually gave way to one of recovery and rebuilding. In July 1948 the hated bread rationing ended, followed in May 1950 by the points system. The de-rationing of tea in October 1952 boosted morale, and the end of sweet rationing early in 1953 was symbolic, causing great rejoicing. The return of bananas was equally significant. Anyone who was a child at that time will remember the first time they saw a banana. Auberon Waugh certainly did. In his autobiography Will This Do? he wrote of his father's greed.

'On one occasion, just after the war, the first consignment of bananas reached Britain. Neither I, my sister Teresa nor my sister Margaret had ever eaten a banana throughout the war, when they were unprocurable, but we had heard all about them as the most delicious taste in the world. When this first consignment arrived, the socialist government decided that every child in the country should be allowed one banana. An army of civil servants issued a library of special banana coupons, and

the great day arrived when my mother came home with three bananas. All three were put on my father's plate, and before the anguished eyes of his children, he poured on cream, which was almost unprocurable, and sugar, which was heavily rationed, and ate all three.'

Fashion was already telling a story of change. When Christian Dior's New Look was first shown in 1947, the long, full skirts seemed a shockingly profligate use of fabric compared to wartime Utility clothes. But by the 1950s the New Look was seen everywhere.

In 1951 the Festival of Britain brought a surge of optimism. The vast exhibition on the South Bank of the Thames in London, celebrated British design and talent in the context of post-war recovery and rebuilding. For children the whole point of the Festival was the fabulous fun-fair in Battersea Park.

On 2 June 1953, Queen Elizabeth was crowned in Westminster Abbey and a new era in history began. At last, putting the war and its deprivations behind them, people looked forward to a little modest self-indulgence.

As far as food was concerned, sugar would not come off the ration until September 1953, and butter, cheese, meat and bacon would still be rationed until the following year. But the rations were more generous than they had been during and immediately after the war. Elizabeth David was already on the path that would change the way the British middle classes cooked and ate, with the publication in 1950 of *Mediterranean Food,* followed in 1951 by *French Country Cooking.*

CONSTANCE SPRY'S CORONATION CHICKEN

Serves 8

Constance Spry, the other great cookery guru of the 1950s and 1960s, was to publish her massive tome in 1954. In it she wrote the recipe for the all-time, iconic party dish: Coronation Chicken. Conceived and first executed to celebrate the coronation of Queen Elizabeth II, it has stood the test of time and can still be encountered on celebratory buffets today. And very welcome it always is.

2 chickens
water and a little wine to cover
1 carrot
a bouquet garni
salt
3–4 peppercorns

for the cream of curry sauce:
1 tablespoon oil
55g (2oz) onion, peeled and finely
  chopped
1 dessertspoon curry powder

1 teaspoon tomato purée
1 glass red wine
¾ glass water
1 bay leaf
salt and freshly ground black pepper
1–2 teaspoons sugar, to taste
1–2 lemon slices
a squeeze of lemon juice
1–2 tablespoons apricot purée
¾ pt mayonnaise
3 tablespoons lightly whipped cream

Poach the chickens, with the carrot, bouquet garni, salt and peppercorns, in a large pan of water and a little wine, enough barely to cover, for about 40 minutes or until tender.

Allow to cool in the liquid. Joint the birds and remove the bones with care.

To make the sauce, heat the oil in a pan, add the onion and cook gently for 3–4 minutes. Add the curry powder and cook again for 1–2 minutes. Add the tomato purée, red wine, water and bay leaf. Bring to the boil, season with salt, pepper and sugar to taste. Add the lemon and lemon juice. Simmer with the pan uncovered 5–10 minutes. Strain and leave to cool.

Add the sauce by degrees to the mayonnaise with the apricot purée to taste. Adjust the seasoning, adding a little more lemon juice if necessary. Finish with 2 tablespoons of whipped cream.

Take a small amount of sauce (enough to coat the chicken) and mix it with the remaining cream and some seasoning. Mix the chicken and the sauce together, arrange on a dish, and coat with the extra sauce.

YOUR COURAGE
YOUR CHEERFULNESS
YOUR RESOLUTION

WILL BRING
US VICTORY

TURN OVER A NEW LEAF

VEGETABLE GROWER'S CALENDAR

When the war ended in 1945 the Dig for Victory campaign was still as vigorous as it had been at the start, and the Ministry of Agriculture published a new set of *Allotment and Garden Guides*, based on monthly tasks and advice. The introduction stated, '...we are out to help you to get better results from your vegetable plot and your fruit garden. Every month we shall try to do three things: first, we shall remind you of the things that ought to have been done, but may not have been possible because of the weather or for some other reason; secondly, we shall deal with gardening operations for the month; thirdly, we shall look ahead a month or two and remind you of what you need to do in readiness.'

The advice was practical and sound. Fashions in gardening techniques come and go, but basic methods don't change much, and it still holds good today.

JANUARY

CARRY ON DIGGING and manuring provided the ground is not too wet. Aim to manure one-third of your land, as part of a three-year crop rotation. This is where you will grow onions, leeks, peas and beans.

PRUNE fruit trees, if not already done.

PLAN for the year ahead. Order seed potatoes and vegetable seeds. Clean and sharpen tools and service machinery.

INSPECT crops you have stored (potatoes, onions, shallots, carrots, beetroots and turnips) every few weeks to make sure they are safe from frost, wet, rats and other enemies. Remove any that show signs of decay.

TIPS:
Never put tools away dirty. Wash off any soil, dry them with an old cloth and wipe with an oily rag before putting them away.
Don't leave tools lying about where they may rust or rot.
Keep tools in good condition by using them often.

SOW BROAD BEANS AND SPINACH.

PLANT SHALLOTS 6in to 9in apart with 1ft between rows, with the tops of the bulbs just showing above ground.

PLANT JERUSALEM ARTICHOKE tubers 6in. deep, 12–15in apart, with 2ft 6in between rows. The plants grow tall and can be used to screen the manure or compost heap.

CHIT POTATOES (see page 63)

PROPAGATE RHUBARB, dividing old roots with a sharp spade or knife so that each piece contains one or two good buds. Plant 2ft apart in deeply-dug, well-manured ground in a sunny spot. Do not harvest stalks from plants divided this year.

MARCH

SOWING AND PLANTING
But don't try to sow seeds when the soil sticks to your boots. Wait for a fine spell when the soil is workable.

SOW PARSNIPS, PEAS, ONIONS, LETTUCES, RADISHES AND PARSLEY in their final positions.

CLEAR AWAY old stumps of Brussels, cabbage etc and prepare the land for a new crop.

LIFT LEEKS to make space for other crops. Eat them or heel them in in a shady place.

DIG the ground where you plan to grow roots. Leave it rough until you are ready to sow.

SOW seeds of Brussels sprouts and leeks in a special seedbed.

PREPARE A SEED BED

1. On a patch about 4ft by 4ft break down all lumps and remove any stones and all roots of grass or weeds.

2. Firm the soil by treading it as soon as it is dry enough not to stick to your boots. Don't stamp it down.

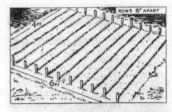

3. Loosen the surface by raking lightly. Place short sticks to mark ends of rows, which should be 6in apart. Stretch string between the sticks.

4. Standing on a board so as not to tread the ground too hard, make shallow drills along the lines with a stick.

5. Sow an even single line of seeds along the bottom of each drill. Cover the seeds lightly with soil. Rake lightly to finish

TIPS:

Never sow peas in wet soil.

Protect the germinating seeds from birds with black cotton stretched on sticks about 6 in. above the soil.

APRIL

SPRING is the busiest time. Seeds are germinating, so are weeds. And it's time to start successional sowings of several crops.

HOE OFTEN to maintain a loose surface mulch and keep down weeds, pushing the hoe to and fro on the surface between rows of crops and on vacant ground.

LAST CHANCE to order tomato plants and Brussels sprout plants for planting out in May or June and to clear away cabbage and other stumps and dig the ground for a following crop.

THE FRUIT GARDEN

Treat your fruit trees and bushes to a spring dressing of bonemeal every few years.

DWARF AND HARICOT BEANS

The plants are tender and should not be sown in the open until mid-April in the south and mid-May in the north. Sow successive batches until mid-July, 9 in apart with 2 ft. between rows. Mulch lightly with lawn mowings, decayed leaves or compost.

BEET

Round shaped varieties mature quickly and are easier to boil in the usual kitchen pot than the longer kinds—a point the missus will appreciate. Sow in April 1-1/2 to 2 in. deep and in rows at least 1 ft. apart. Sow seeds in small clusters 6 in. apart, and thin the plants to one when three leaves have formed. Stretch black cotton above the rows to protect the seedlings from birds.

CABBAGES

For a late summer crop, sow a row in the seedbed now (see March Guide).

CARROTS

Make a first sowing in early April. In May or early June sow a crop to store for winter use. Thinnings may be pulled and used as early carrots but the ground should be firmed again after thinning out, to reduce the danger of carrot fly attack. A late sowing in mid-July will provide tender young carrots for use the following spring (April—May). Sow thinly, 1in deep in rows 1ft apart. To avoid wasting seed, mix it with a little dry earth or sand before sowing.

LETTUCE

Sow a short row ½in deep every fortnight.

PEAS

Sow maincrop peas in April. As soon as peas have three pairs of leaves, they are ready for sticking. Don't cross the two rows of sticks at the top, as this makes the plants get tangled in a mass; stick them firmly in the ground upright. (Today plastic or wire netting stretched vertically between canes can be used instead of sticks.)

POTATOES

Plant varieties other than "earlies".

SPINACH

The Ministry's cropping plan provides for inter-cropping three rows of dwarf peas with two of spinach. Sow 1in deep and 15in apart. On light soils summer spinach runs to seed quickly unless well watered.

SWISS CHARD

Sow as for spinach.

ONIONS

Gradually harden off plants raised in the greenhouse and plant in rows 6 in apart, with 1ft between rows. Set each bulb just on top of the ground and press the soil firmly around its roots.

RADISHES

Sow little and often, very thinly to avoid having to thin the seedlings.

TIP:

If you sow a few radish seeds with onions, carrots and beet (one seed every 6in) they will grow quickly and show you the line before the other seeds germinate. Hoeing and weeding can then begin earlier.

MAY

KEEP ON HOEING AND HAND WEEDING.

CONTINUE to make successional sowings of crops to harvest in summer and autumn.

THIN SEEDLINGS

When the ground is moist and the weather cool with showers forecast, thin out lettuces, spinach and parsnips. If the weather is dry, water thoroughly before and after thinning. Pull out the weakest seedlings, leaving the strongest to grow on.

EARTH UP POTATOES (see Potato Pete, page 61)

MULCH PEAS AND BEANS with compost or lawn clippings to prevent weeds and conserve moisture.

Winter greens: sprouting broccoli, winter cabbage
and kale.

SOW RUNNER BEANS AND MARROWS in the open.
Provide each runner bean plant with a stout,
straight stake 6–8ft long, without branches or twigs.
Make two rows of stakes slanted to cross at the top,
allowing for a cross stake to be fixed.

PLANT OUT BRUSSELS SPROUTS.

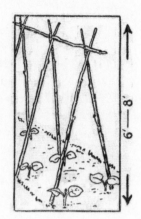

JUNE

CARRY ON WEEDING and water in dry spells, specially runner beans.

WATCH OUT for Cabbage White butterflies' caterpillars on brassicas, pick
them off and destroy them.

SOW SWEDES AND CELERIAC in shallow drills 18in apart.. Celeriac needs
plenty of water in dry weather. Remove side shoots as they appear and
hoe regularly.

PLANT OUT CELERY
1. Dig a trench 18in wide and 1ft deep, fork manure or compost into the
bottom and replace soil to within 2in of ground level.
2. Set the plants 10in apart in staggered double rows, 1ft apart.
3. Water them in and give plenty of water in dry weather.

PLANT OUT TOMATOES when the danger of frost is past. A sunny,
sheltered south or south-west facing wall or fence is the ideal spot
(see p70).

PINCH OUT growing tips of runner beans when they reach the top of
their poles.

CARRY ON WEEDING, THINNING OUT, WATERING

In a dry summer you may need to choose which plants to water and which must take their chance. Newly transplanted seedlings are first in line. Runner beans may not develop pods if they are too dry. Then come celery, marrows (courgettes) and tomatoes. A good soaking once a week is better than a sprinkle every day.

MULCH PEAS AND BEANS with grass mowings or compost to a depth of 1 in. along each side of the rows to conserve moisture.

PLANT OUT LEEKS when the seedlings are 6in high.
1. If the soil is dry, soak the seedbed before lifting. Cut off the tips of the leaves, lift carefully with a fork and plant 9in apart with 12 to 18in between rows.
2. With a dibber make holes at least 6 in. deep.
3. Drop a plant into each hole.
4. Water in to wash soil round the roots, but don't fill the hole with soil.

SOW

Make final sowings of lettuce, spring onions, beetroots, peas and carrots. Late-sown carrots usually escape the attention of the carrot fly.

CARRY ON COMPOSTING

As well as kitchen waste put pea stems, potato haulms, outside lettuce leaves and grass cuttings on the compost heap.

PLANT OUT CABBAGES AND OTHER BRASSICAS. In dry weather, give the seed-bed a good soaking the night before. Lift the young plants carefully with a fork, with as much soil as possible adhering to the roots. Water each hole before and after planting.

PERSONALISE A MARROW Scratch children's initials (or your own) on courgettes while they are small, and leave them to grow huge. The names will grow with them.

AUGUST

DRY HERBS
Pick shoots of thyme, sage, mint, marjoram, tarragon and parsley just before they flower. Tie into bundles, wash them, cover with muslin to keep out dust and hang to dry in an airy shed or near the fire. Store away from the light.

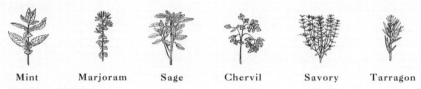

| Mint | Marjoram | Sage | Chervil | Savory | Tarragon |

FREEZE HERBS
Strip off the leaves and freeze them in small plastic bags.

LAST CHANCE TO SOW SPRING CABBAGE. Don't sow it where earlier sowings of cabbage were made as the soil may contain Cabbage Root Fly or the spores of Club Root. Sow late kale now for a green crop in March and April. Thin as required during growth.

PREPARE THE GROUND for autumn sowings of winter lettuce and turnips. Sow a week or two later.

HARVEST SHALLOTS when the leaves start to wither. Lift the bulbs and leave on a dry surface, such as a path for a few days, to ripen and dry them. Tie into bundles or lay in trays or boxes, and store in a dry, frost-proof, airy shed. Look them over from time to time and throw out any decaying bulbs

Pinch out here

TOMATOES
'Stop' the plants by pinching out the main growing shoot just above the fourth truss. Water and feed regularly. Let the sun get at the fruit by thinning out the leaves to expose developing trusses.

FRUIT GARDEN
Summer fruiting raspberries, blackberries and loganberries should be pruned as soon as the last fruit is picked. Cut all canes that have borne fruit down to ground level and burn the canes. Tie the new canes to supporting wires, 5 or 6in apart using string.

HARVEST AND STORE the fruits of your labours.

POTATOES
1. About a fortnight before lifting, cut the leafy stems off and remove.
2. Lift the potatoes carefully with a fork and leave them on the ground to dry for about four or five hours.
3. Throw away any damaged or diseased potatoes.
4. Store in boxes or barrels lined thickly with old newspapers to protect against frost.
6. Keep in a dry, frost-proof shed and cover them with old sacking.
7. For storing outdoors in a clamp, see diagram below.

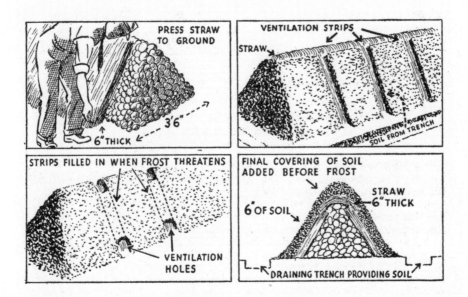

HARICOT BEANS
When the pods begin turning brown, pull up the plants, tie in bundles and hang in a dry, open shed to ripen. When quite dry, shell out the seeds and store in boxes in a cold, frost-proof place.

MAKE AN ONION ROPE

1. Remove roots, loose skin and most of the tops of the onions.

2. Hang up a rope about 3ft long, with a knot at the end, and tie a single good-sized onion to the end to serve as a base.

3. Starting from the base, tie on four onions at a time, arranging them round the rope and holding in position with one hand, while you wind string round to secure them.

4. Tie the string securely and cut off the onion tops as you go.

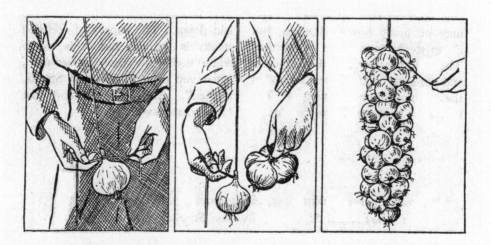

MARROWS AND PUMPKINS

Store in a warm dry place where the temperature will not fall below 7°C (45°F), such as a kitchen, bedroom or attic. Store the fruits on shelves, or hang from the ceiling in nets. They will keep well beyond Halloween, until January or February.

PLANT OUT SPRING CABBAGES 1ft apart with 1ft 6in to 2ft between rows.

TIP:

Don't let parsley run to seed. Cut the plants almost to ground level and water them to provide fresh leaves through the winter.

OCTOBER

STORE CARROTS
Lift the roots carefully with a fork, taking care not to damage them. Trim off the leaves near the crown, but do not cut the top part of the carrot, even if it is green. In one or more boxes put a layer of dry sand or soil over the bottom then a layer of carrots, another layer of sand and so on until the box is full.

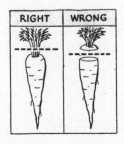

STORE BEETROOTS
Lift before frost seriously threatens. Twist off the leaves (don't cut them) and bury in boxes of damp sand. Keep in a frost-proof shed or cellar.

JERUSALEM ARTICHOKES keep better in the ground. Cut down the stems and heap bracken or leaves over the roots.

PICK BRUSSELS SPROUTS. Always start at the bottom of the stem and work upwards.

FORCE RHUBARB. When the plants have shed their summer leaves, place some dry leaves or bracken loosely over the crowns then cover with a box or big pot. This encourages the rhubarb to make early growth.

TIP:
Draw up a little soil round leek plants to encourage sizeable, well-blanched stems.

NOVEMBER

CLEAN UP DEBRIS. Leaves, etc. harbour pests, so pick them up and compost or burn them.

DIG all unoccupied ground, turning over rough clods so the frost can break them down.

PLANT FRUIT TREES

In theory you can plant any time between late autumn and the end of March, but in practice the longer you wait the more you are likely to be delayed by frost, snow, or soil too wet to work. Peaches and pears must have sun. Other fruits do best in sun, but tolerate partial shade. So plant peaches or pears on a south wall or fence, apples and plums on the west or east, and morello cherries on the north. Black currants, gooseberries and raspberries should be netted against bird attack.

1. Dig a planting hole at least 2ft wide and deep. Fork over the subsoil before laying in a bucketful of manure or compost.
2. Hammer in a stake to support the tree. Check the tree's roots, cut off any damaged parts and untangle twisted roots.
3. Put the tree in the hole at the same depth as it was in the nursery and spread the roots out evenly.
4. Half cover the roots with soil. Give the tree a shake so the soil settles.
5. Tread it firm, add the remaining soil and tread again.
6. Tie the tree to the stake and mulch the root area with farmyard manure or compost.

DECEMBER

FEED THE BIRDS
You need to keep them fit so they can devour next year's pests.

TAKE A REST FROM THE GARDEN OR ALLOTMENT
Put on your slippers, put your feet up, study your seed catalogue and dream of bigger and sweeter crops to come.

YOUR VICTORY GARDEN
counts more than ever!

Cookery Calendar

SEASONAL WEEKLY MENUS

One of the secrets of thrifty family meals is planning ahead. Another is making the best use of seasonal ingredients, because they are cheaper than foods flown in from distant countries, in terms of both their monetary cost and their environmental cost.

The thinking behind these weekly plans is that meat is a weekend treat but even so, need not be expensive, and that a mid-week chicken will provide a second meal plus plenty of flavoursome stock for soups and stews. Other meals can consist mainly of potatoes, rice, beans or lentils, cooked in a meaty sauce or stock left from an earlier meal and accompanied by seasonal vegetables and salads.

The following weekly meal plans show you how to follow these two principals. A main meal is suggested for each day, and lunch as well as supper for weekends. The week starts on Sunday, the day of the traditional roast joint.

Breakfast is usually fruit juice and cereal (if people can be persuaded to love porridge, so much the better), wholemeal bread or toast, or oatcakes. Teatime treats might include carrot cake, chocolate brownies and flapjacks, made at a family baking session at the weekend.

For weekday lunch, those at home could choose from home-made vegetable soup; baked potatoes; bubble and squeak; tomatoes; mushrooms or sardines on toast; Welsh rabbit, varied to suit individual tastes or the changing seasons.

SPRING

SUNDAY

LUNCH
Roast shoulder of lamb; roast potatoes; spring greens with ginger and garlic.
Pineapple upside-down cake (p199)

SUPPER
Split pea soup (Crème Ambassadeur) (109), Cheese with damson preserve.

MONDAY
Cheesy leek and potato gratin (pxx); peas with bacon lardons.
Apple purée with Greek yoghurt and brown sugar.

TUESDAY
Shepherd's pie made with remains of Sunday joint (p159–62); cole slaw salad.
Rhubarb baked in orange juice; beetroot chocolate brownies (p150).

WEDNESDAY
Rabbit casserole (p156); mashed potato; purple sprouting broccoli with salsa verde.
Orange and banana fruit salad.

THURSDAY
Egg and bacon tart (p132), garlicky spinach; carrot cake (p124)

FRIDAY
Savoury pancakes filled with mushrooms and chopped rabbit or chicken from Wednesday's casserole (p156); ruby chard (leaves and stalks cooked separately) steamed and sautéed with onion, garlic and orange juice; rhubarb fool with brandy snaps (p186)

SATURDAY

LUNCH
Kedgeree; watercress, rocket and orange salad.
Gooseberry crumble (using bottled gooseberries p43), Vanilla ice cream.

SUPPER
Nettle soup (p31) with wholemeal bread (p137); potato floddies (p145) with home-made jam and crème fraiche.

SUMMER

SUNDAY
LUNCH
Family party: Spiced beef (p113),
new potatoes, baby broad beans;
raspberry trifle

SUPPER
Devilled eggs (p179), leafy salad;
cheese and biscuits with Hugh's
Glutney (p26).

MONDAY
Risotto with peas and beans;
strawberries and cream.

TUESDAY
Pasta with meaty sauce (spiced
beef from Sunday's lunch, chopped
and mixed with onions, carrots and
tomato purée); cheese and grapes.

WEDNESDAY
Kidneys in red wine (p115), mashed
potato, French beans; peach and
raspberry tart.

THURSDAY
Toad in the hole (p96), baby carrots
and broad beans; summer fruit
salad (p182)

FRIDAY
Rabbit or chicken pie (p30), new
potatoes, runner beans; fresh fruit.

SATURDAY
LUNCH
Roast chicken with bread sauce;
new potatoes, French beans and
beetroots; summer pudding.

SUPPER
Courgette soufflé (p123), wholemeal
bread (p137); blackcurrant ice
cream.

AUTUMN

SUNDAY
LUNCH
Boiled beef with carrots and dumplings (p160); blackberry and apple pudding (p33).

SUPPER
Vegetable soup (Household Soup, p104); fresh fruit jelly.

MONDAY
Bread and cheese pudding (p118) with fresh tomato sauce; stewed plums.

TUESDAY
Cold beef with spiced peaches (p44), baked potatoes, leafy salad

WEDNESDAY
Roast carrots, parsnips and beetroots. Blackberry sorbet.

THURSDAY
Mock fish pie (artichoke gratin p143); courgettes; goat's cheese with ripe pears.

FRIDAY
Herring fillets fried in oatmeal (p94) with gooseberry sauce, mashed butternut squash; apple snow.

SATURDAY
LUNCH
Stuffed and rolled breast of lamb (p159); mock apricot flan (p148)

SUPPER
Welsh Rabbit with a poached egg on top, leafy salad. Fresh fruit.

WINTER

SUNDAY

LUNCH

Lancashire hotpot (p92), pear upside-down cake (see pineapple recipe p199).

SUPPER

Champ (p145) with crispy bacon rashers; fresh fruit.

MONDAY

Mock Duck (sausage and apple) (p142); curly kale; damson fool.

TUESDAY

Calves liver alla Veneziana; mashed potato; winter fruit salad.

WEDNESDAY

Hotpot broth (Sunday's hotpot leftovers chopped small with lentils or pearl barley and chopped fresh herbs added); apple crumble.

THURSDAY

Pigs in clover (p144), garlicky Savoy cabbage; Cranachan made with bottled or frozen raspberries.

FRIDAY

Curried vegetables (see lamb curry p169) with rice and pickles; Cheddar with damson cheese.

SATURDAY

LUNCH

Gammon and spinach; baked potatoes; vanilla ice cream with Granny Lascelles' fudge sauce (p127).

SUPPER

Bubble and squeak with gammon; mince pies (p184)

Acknowledgements

I owe a huge debt to the staff of the Imperial War Museum. Knowing that I can rely on their knowledge and enthusiasm has helped me enormously throughout the research for and writing of this book. I am especially grateful to Terry Charman and James Taylor, the Museum's historians in the Research & Information Department who, in spite of being extremely busy with research for the Ministry of Food exhibition have given up precious time to help me with my research. I owe particular thanks to Terry for checking the text of the book.

I would also like specially to thank Elizabeth Bowers and Abigail Ratcliffe in the Publishing Department, and Madeleine James who organised all the photography and picture ordering for the book; Angela Godwin and Laura Whalley, Emma Goodrum and all those staff in the Collecting Department's who went to great lengths to assemble archive material including the art work that makes the book such a pleasure to look at and the Photographic Studio for supplying the images. I'd also like to give thanks to Company of Cooks (www.companyofcooks.com).

The Museum's archives supplied most of the material I needed but the following books have also been invaluable sources of information:

Nella Last's War: A Mother's Diary 1939-45, Ed. Richard Broad & Suzie Fleming, Profile 2005

Good Eating, Suggestions for Wartime Dishes, *Daily Telegraph*, re-issued by Macmillan 2006

Colyton at War, ed Geoff Elliott, Colyton Parish History Society

Private Battles: How The War Almost Defeated Us, Simon Garfield, Ebury Press 2006

We are at War: The Remarkable Diaries of Five Ordinary People in Extraordinary Times, Simon Garfield

Land at War: The Official Story of British Farming 1939-1944, London HMSO 1945

Our Longest Days: A People's History of the Second World War, Ed. Sandra Koa Wing, Profile Books

Digging for Victory: Wartime Gardening with Mr Middleton, CH Middleton, George Allen and Unwin 1942

Austerity Britain 1945-51, David Kynaston, Bloomsbury 2007

Feeding the Nation, Marguerite Patten OBE, Hamlyn and the Imperial War Museum 2005

The BBC's 'WW2 People's War' online archive has been a valuable source of wartime memories contributed by members of the public and gathered by the BBC. The archive can be found at www.bbc.co.uk/ww2peopleswar . Among their contributors I am grateful to Marjory Heaton and Pauline Colcutt of The Fernhurst Centre, Frank Mee, and Gwen Millward.

I'd also like to thank everyone at Hodder's who worked on the book: Nicky Ross and Sarah Hammond for their support throughout, Katey Mackenzie for her sympathetic and unobtrusive editing, Camilla Dowse, a tireless and brilliant Picture Researcher, Georgia Vaux for her marvellously evocative design, Bill Jones in Production, and Karen Geary in Publicity.

Tony Ross kindly allowed me to quote from his wartime letters from his fiancée Joan Charles. Sylvia Gibb, Lyla Harling, Peter Boggis, Jennie Hope-Bradshaw and other friends were generous with their reminiscences, and I'm especially grateful to Kath Leadbeater for allowing me to use material from her father Kenneth Thornton Roberts' war-time army recipe book and from her own book, *When it's Brown it's Done*.

I also thank The British Records Association for permission to use an extract from Sources for the History of London 1939-45; Pam Corbin for recipes from *Preserves: River Cottage Handbook No.2*; Curtis Brown Ltd, London on behalf of the Trustees of the Mass Observation archive for permission to quote from the Archive, Copyright © The Trustees of the Mass Observation Archive; Geoff Elliott and Colyton Parish History Society for permission to quote extracts from *Colyton at War* by Geoff Elliott Copyright © Geoff Elliott 200; Hugh Fearnley-Whittingstall for recipes from *The River Cottage Cookbook* and *River Cottage Every Day*; The Imperial War Museum for permission to quote from their archives; Fiona Nevile-Bowles for permission to publish the recipe for Stuffed, Rolled Breast of Lamb from www.CottageSmallholder.com; Marguerite Patten and the Imperial War Museum for recipes from *Feeding the Nation*; Persephone Books (www. Persephonebooks.co.uk) for permission to quote from *They Can't Ration These* by Vicomte de Maudit; PFD (www.pfd.co.uk) on behalf of the Estate of Auberon Waugh for permission to reproduce an excerpt from *Will This Do* © Auberon Waugh 1991.

PICTURE ACKNOWLEDGEMENTS

IMPERIAL WAR MUSEUM:
Image references: 6 (PST0671), 8 (PST2814), 10 (K037191),
12 (PST14914), 15 (PST6078 detail), 17 (PST15775), 18 (PST0200),
19 (PST016627), 22 (PST0146), 26 (PST0143), 29 (PST0129),
34 (PST0696), 36 (PST2893), 39 (PST8411), 40 (PST14776), 41
(PST14742), 42 (PST17001), 44 (K037261), 47 (K0372611), 49
(K930005161), 50 (K9113091), 52 (PST0102), 54 (PST2916), 56
(K037031), 60 (PST20611), 61 (PST3366), 62 (K0321391), 64
(PST8105), 65 (PST6015), 67 (K971496), 71 (PST016992), 74-75
(PST17019), 79 (PST20697), 80 (PST14757), 81 (PST0726), 82
(PST4944), 83 (EPH4927), 84 (PST3108), 88 (K04133113), 91
(EPH5742), 93 (PST20687), 95 (EPH57302), 97 (K03714), 98
(EPH1703), 99 (K0413321), 100 (EPH1705), 105 (PST6080), 106
(K979671), 110 (PST0743), 112 (K0321282), 116 (PST20675), 117
(EPH5924), 118 (K037171), 120 (K971495), 121 (K0757651), 122
(K03717), 123 (K093194), 125 (PST0068), 126 (K037251), 127
(EPH0377), 129 (K0321173), 132 (EPH9482), 133 (EPH9737),
134 (K0321281), 135 (K037171), 136 (PST20684), 138 (K046301),
139 (K82581), 147 (PST3448), 149 (K037261), 152 (PST3454), 153
(K037261), 157 (K861693), 158 (K78513), 161 (K94424), 163 (K008740),
165 (EPH5729), 166 (K9918852), 169 (EPH2490), 170 (K0315724),
172 (K0757652), 178 (PST8117), 190 (K9918851), 195 (K9624301), 196
(K06771016), 197 top & bottom (K06771017), 198 top (K06771027),
bottom (K06771032), 199 top (K06771033), bottom (K06771042),
202 (K06771054), 203 (K06771073), 204 top (K0677112), bottom
(K06771083), 205 (K06771092), 206 (K06771093), 207 top (K06771102),
bottom (K0677111), 208 top (K06771107), bottom (K06771058), 210
(K08518301), 211 (K093193), 214 (K9624272)

ADDITIONAL PICTURE SOURCES:
Courtesy of The Advertising Archives: 141. © Mary Evans Picture
Library/ Alamy: 108, 155. © K.J. Historical/ Corbis: 209. © TopFoto: 193.
© The National Archives / HIP / TopFoto: 21, 72. Private Collections: 77,
94, 114, 130, 183, 186, 188, 212-213. Courtesy of the Savoy Archives: 87.

Every reasonable effort has been made to contact the copyright holders, but if there are any errors or omissions, Hodder & Stoughton will
be pleased to insert the appropriate acknowledgement in any subsequent
printing of this publication.

INDEX